UNDERSTANDING SOCIETY

This poignant book examines poverty, wealth and inequality in the UK, and provides insight into its history, its present-day forms and possible routes to its eradication.

The book demonstrates how poverty, wealth and inequality are constructed in the UK, noting that it is not an innate part of the human experience, but a phenomenon which is constructed by economic and social circumstances. Using work ranging from Malthus' interrogation of the '*natural right of the poor to full support in [...] society*' to more contemporary economic approaches, including Thomas Picketty's *Capitalism in the Twenty First Century*, the authors examine various forms of poverty, wealth and inequality in the UK, using the UK Household Longitudinal Study, Understanding Society, dataset to ground their findings in quantitative evidence. The book concludes with an assessment of what is required to potentially end poverty in the UK, and a call to apply evidence-based research to the reshaping of social policy in the UK.

This book is an excellent resource for students, policy makers and lecturers seeking a greater understanding of poverty, wealth and inequality in the UK. It will be of particular interest to those working in or studying the fields of human geography, economics and social policy.

Carlo J. Morelli is Senior Lecturer in Economics at the University of Dundee Business School, UK.

Paul T. Seaman was a Lecturer in Economics at the University of Dundee Business School, UK.

UNDERSTANDING SOCIETY

Poverty, Wealth and Inequality in the UK

Carlo J. Morelli and Paul T. Seaman

Routledge
Taylor & Francis Group
LONDON AND NEW YORK

Cover credit: © Getty Images

First published 2022
by Routledge
4 Park Square, Milton Park, Abingdon, Oxon OX14 4RN

and by Routledge
605 Third Avenue, New York, NY 10158

Routledge is an imprint of the Taylor & Francis Group, an informa business

British Library Cataloguing-in-Publication Data
A catalogue record for this book is available from the British Library

Library of Congress Cataloging-in-Publication Data
Names: Morelli, Carlo J., author. | Seaman, Paul T., author.
Title: Understanding society: poverty, wealth and inequality in the UK/ Carlo J. Morelli and Paul T. Seaman.
Description: Abingdon, Oxon; New York, NY: Routledge, 2022. |
Includes bibliographical references and index. |
Identifiers: LCCN 2021045514 (print) | LCCN 2021045515 (ebook) |
Classification: LCC HC260.P6 M67 2022 (print) | LCC HC260.P6 (ebook) |
DDC 362.50941–dc23
LC record available at https://lccn.loc.gov/2021045514
LC ebook record available at https://lccn.loc.gov/2021045515

ISBN: 978-1-138-89442-6 (hbk)
ISBN: 978-1-138-89444-0 (pbk)
ISBN: 978-1-315-17995-7 (ebk)

DOI: 10.4324/9781315179957

Typeset in Bembo
by KnowledgeWorks Global Ltd.

Paul Timothy Seaman 19th March 1968 – 18th March 2019

and

Mary Morelli 19th October 1933 – 5th April 2020 and
Vera Joyce Seaman 22nd August 1935 – 12th July 2020

CONTENTS

TABLES

FIGURES

BOX

ACKNOWLEDGEMENTS

This book should be understood as a celebration and memorial to my co-author Dr. Paul Timothy Seaman. Without his commitment and skill in data modelling, this work would not have been possible but tragically, before its completion, Paul passed away and he was not able to see the final manuscript.

Paul and I had a long friendship which began shortly after we both joined the Economic Studies Department at Dundee University. Our extensive research collaboration examining poverty, inequality and social policy lasted some 15 years. Our first academic paper, published in 2005 was followed by nearly a dozen further papers and book chapters. Paul's contribution, as an economist, was always to focus upon the means through which longitudinal data could be utilised to examine issues of inequality at the household level.

Paul had a very sharp intellect which could dissect a problem and consider how an economic analysis could be brought to bare on the question such that it could be empirically tested with data, initially from the British Household Panel dataset and later on with the United Kingdom Longitudinal Household Panel dataset.

Our regular discussions over coffee, in my case, and sweetened cider, in his, often took the form of an exited discussion over the minutiae of data and its applicability to the questions we were considering. For those who joined us and attempted to join in the discussion, they very quickly abandoned any attempt to engage with the pair of us.

While we always held highly divergent views, we were able to develop a long-lasting research collaboration due to our mutual respect for one another's contribution to our work and a willingness to be challenged by the evidence, as it developed through our research.

Thanks must also go to the editors and editorial assistants at our publishers Routledge, in particular Claire Jarvis and Catherine Jones. Without Claire and Catherine's sympathy and understanding of the circumstances behind the many delays in this work, it would never have seen the light of day.

Carlo Morelli, July 2021

1

INTRODUCTION

Understanding society: poverty, wealth and inequality in the UK

Introduction

This book seeks to use the Understanding Society, UK Household Longitudinal Study survey (UKHLS) dataset to examine the extent and characteristics of poverty, wealth and inequality in the UK. In doing so the book provides students, policymakers and academic lecturers and researchers with an assessment from the Understanding Society dataset and disseminates policy-focused research and new thinking to highlight the advantages of, largely underutilised, longitudinal research methodologies.

Inequality, wealth and poverty surround our daily lives. In the week of the 30th April 2018 when we first started researching this book, the news of Amber Rudd MP's resignation as Home Office Minister was the first item on the news, as a result of the racially motivated inequalities faced by the Windrush generation of Commonwealth migrants, in relation to government immigration policy (Financial Times, 2018, p. 1). This was followed by news of the extent to which the British overseas territories act as tax havens for the laundering of 'dirty money'. Estimate of £68 bn from Russia alone is suggested to have passed through the British Virgin Islands before being invested 'legally' in property and other assets (Guardian, 2018, pp. 1–4). Finally, the Scottish Government introduced new legislation imposing a minimum price of alcohol to address alcohol-related poverty and ill health (Herald, 2018, p. 1). Some three years on these three events will have been largely forgotten but could be replaced by the recognition of the failures of COP26 climate change conference to address the impact of climate change on the global south (Financial Times, 2021), the uproar of the return to sleaze and corruption of MPs in the House of Commons (Guardian, 2021, p. 1) and the impact the withdrawal of additional £20 per week support for low-income households through Universal Credit (BBC, 2021). By the time

DOI: 10.4324/9781315179957-1

readers are reading this three almost identical examples of inequality, wealth and poverty in the press could be found if we take a moment to look.

While poverty is the everyday lived experience of vast numbers of the population in the UK, at the same time a tiny minority have levels of personal wealth beyond what most individuals would find possible to comprehend. As a result we often seek measures of income inequality which place the scale of inequality into recognisable and understandable forms. Pen's Parade was used to illustrate the levels of income inequality in which the population of a country is suggested to walk past a single spot during one hour (Pen, 1974). The original parade illustrated that it is not until 48 minutes into the hour that we will see individuals pass the spot who are of average height, before then all that can be observed is a vast stream of stunted and reduced height individuals. Even median income individuals are only half the height of the average. However, just five minutes before, the end giants begin to appear, and in the last minute individuals who are miles high end the parade (Colbeck, 2010). Similarly, as with other forms of inequality our understanding requires means by which the data can be brought down to a recognisable level. So, the Fawcett Society's use of 'Equal Pay Day', the day when women cease to be paid relative to male earnings as a means to illustrate gender pay inequalities. In the UK, 20th November 2020 was calculated to be Equal Pay Day, despite being 50 years since the introduction of the 1970 Equal Pay Act (Fawcett Society, 2020). Finally, we demonstrate how falling life expectancy across a city can be depicted by the distance walked, a number of traffic lights passed or tube stations travelled to represent years lost in life expectancy between the wealthiest and poorest areas in communities that exist cheek by jowl to one another (O'Brien, 2014).

Inequality and wealth

Poverty, for decades, has been the focus of attention for academics from across a range of social science disciplines. A veritable industry exists ranging from research networks, policy institutes and campaigning charitable organisations, whose aim is the creation of a wider and deeper understanding of the existence and experience of poverty both in the UK and the wider world. Demand from the non-governmental sector to listen to, and frame policy from, the perspective of those facing poverty has been a persistent conclusion from those working with and representing disadvantaged and excluded populations.

A key difficulty with this focus upon poverty, however, has been the emphasis within social policy of seeking to address the condition of those facing poverty. Poverty research seeks to identify the characteristics and uniqueness of this sub-group of the population, to determine the vulnerabilities, predispositions and inter-relationships within society that places this group at risk of poverty. While this may derive from a sympathetic rather than punitive perspective, this research nevertheless is indicative of a focus upon deficiency, deviance and 'othering' as an intellectual basis. Inequality, by contrast, examines the totality of a social hierarchy in which the basis for the hierarchy's existence is the focus of attention.

A largely new found focus upon inequality and wealth has required a shift in the approach undertaken by academic scholars who were previously dominated by the question of poverty, to the almost exclusion of inequality. Barriers to movement within a hierarchy, social immobility, structural impediment and differential advantage are now the intellectual starting point for study. Concepts of deficiency, deviance and 'othering' are rarely applied to those populations who are the beneficiaries of income inequalities. Remedial action for the disadvantaged minority at the bottom of society may still be a policy outcome of such research, but now it is within a broader question of addressing the structural nature of poverty and addressing the injustice of inequality that is the context of such work. The emergence of this structural nature of inequality and poverty can also be readily identified by a historical examination of its origins.

Inequality and poverty in historical context

> The existence of a tendency in mankind to increase, if unchecked, beyond the possibility of an adequate supply of food in a limited territory, must at once determine the question as to the natural right of the poor to full support in a state of society where the law of property is recognised.
>
> *(Malthus, 1964, p. 55)*

Thomas Malthus, nineteenth century political philosopher, arguably provides the most important starting point for the study of poverty and inequality in contemporary capitalism. The primary reason for this is that, as his quote above highlights, one of the most central, yet un-debated, tenants of the poverty literature is that poverty is a state of human existence which has always existed in all human society and that poverty and inequality can only therefore be ameliorated, but never eradicated, as part of a wider gradualist process of economic development. As Malthus maintains, there is a natural tendency in mankind to generate demand which is beyond the potential for its satisfaction. Therefore, let us start with a heresy; poverty and inequality have not always existed. The concept of poverty can only emerge with the rise of an economic system for two reasons. Either society generates insufficient resources to permit all individuals to avoid poverty or alternatively a society emerges with sufficient resources, but this wealth and income is concentrated in the hands of a minority at the expense of the majority.

As the twentieth century demonstrates the Malthusian population trap of rising population outpacing the growth of world, output has been discredited leading to an understanding that poverty has been socially constructed by the choices of individuals and institutions to facilitate a specific form of inequality. That earlier societies did not have access to the forms of human wealth available to later human societies cannot be used as a measure of the poverty in any specific society. Just because an ancient slave owner or their slave, or a feudal Lord or their serf, did not have access to an automobile, a mobile phone or antibiotics does not make the entire population of earlier societies poor (Flannery and

Marcus, 2012). All poverty therefore is a relative assessment of the disparity that exists within a society at any given point in time. Thus, any statement we make about poverty must be contextualised within the historical developments of the period under consideration.

In starting with this point, we follow the criticism of Malthus that has been available since his original *Essay on the Principle of Population as It Affects the Future Improvement of Society* was published dating from Ricardo and Marx. As Engels (1996) writing in 1844 notes in the *Outlines of a Critique of Political Economy*, 'if Malthus had not taken such a one–sided view of the matter, he could not have missed seeing that surplus population or labour power is always bound up with surplus wealth, surplus capital and surplus landed property' (Meek, 1953, p. 60). Thus, the critique of the Malthusian law of population was one which located poverty within the structural organisation of modern economies and therefore derived from inequality rather than lack of resources. This point is made much later in the twentieth century in the critique of the more modern economic concept of 'effective demand' in which a contemporary Malthusian limit is reinvented to explain poverty. As Meek, writing in the 1950s, again points out 'an important part of Keynesian theory of effective demand has been made to play a role just as reactionary as that which Malthus intended the original theory [of population] to play' (1954, p. 21).

When examining poverty and inequality, we are undertaking an examination of the structures in society that generate inequalities and as a result poverty. A key consideration is then that poverty can only exist where a hierarchy of power emerges within the specific social relations of society ensuring that poverty not simply emerges but is enforceable over time.

An examination of inequality is then to recognise the institutional structures within society which are necessary for the creation of poverty. Poverty becomes the individual representation of inequality within any specific set of institutional arrangements and is absolute in all its forms. Social exclusion and lack of access to resources becomes the lived experience of those in poverty and is felt in absolute, rather than in relative terms, by those facing poverty. Neither poverty nor inequality are therefore a product of human nature but instead are products of the specific form of economic development a society has created. Therefore, poverty and inequality needs to be understood and placed within its own historic and institutional context. One central underlying theme, in this study, is the examination of the forms of inequality created and re-constructed over time and to examine how even minor changes in the institutional structures of society can impact on inequality and poverty.

Contemporary recognition of inequality

The recent revival of interest in inequality, as opposed to poverty, within academic research follows on from the publication of two highly popular and influential books. The first by Richard Wilkinson and Kate Pickett (2009),

The Spirit Level: Why More Equal Societies Almost Always Do Better, and the second by Thomas Piketty (2014), *Capital in the Twenty First Century*. Together these volumes brought academic evidence to a wide readership of a growing phenomenon which had deep roots within contemporary advanced capitalism, namely a rapid increase in income inequality. Wilkinson and Pickett drew attention to the correlation between national levels of income inequality and a diverse range of social and health inequalities, including addiction, interpersonal violence and imprisonment rates, life expectancy, infant mortality and obesity. Crucially, Wilkinson and Pickett demonstrated that these correlations were consistent internationally such that the greater the levels of income inequality, the greater the negative effects of these social and health problems. As the subtitle of their book identified, it provided an analysis which explained why more equal societies almost always do better. Wilkinson and Pickett's central explanation for the linkage between economic and social dislocation with income inequality derived from their hypothesis that trust, anxiety and socio-evaluative comparison is central to human well-being at a societal level. Inequality and social hierarchy increases recognition of inferiority and a social sense of lack of value for individuals leading to higher levels of stress hormones, evidenced by cortisone levels, in the human body. Higher stress and anxiety leading to higher cortisone levels provides a biological transmission by which social conditions impact on individual biology leading to worsening health and social outcomes (Wilkinson and Pickett, 2009, pp. 31–45). Importantly, for Wilkinson and Pickett in their subsequent work these outcomes impacted on those at the top of the hierarchy as well as the bottom, and thus the impact of inequality could be identified throughout the population relative to more equal societies (Wilkinson and Pickett, 2019).

The economist Thomas Piketty's focus has been the rise in income inequality and capital income ratios for the top income deciles with specific reference to the last quarter of the twentieth century. Piketty's (2014) exhaustive study of advanced economies demonstrates that income inequalities fell during the first half of the twentieth century, reaching their minimum in the period from the Second World War through to the end of the long boom in the early 1970s, and then rose rapidly in the era of neo-liberalism in the last two decades of the twentieth century. Rising income inequalities have then returned to levels not seen since the period before the First World War, and for some economies since the late nineteenth century. As with Wilkinson and Pickett, Piketty's central thesis, however, is not simply that income inequality has risen but that as a result of these developments, fundamental and far-reaching changes in economies are underway. While Wilkinson and Pickett consider rising social and medical problems arising from income inequality, Piketty focuses upon the economic changes in economies underpinning these inequalities. Piketty thus identifies the development of a 'Patrimonial capitalism' emerging whereby the stock of wealth rather than the flow of income is the primary determinant of the continued dominance of the top 1% of the world's population. Piketty demonstrates that it is the rising capital/income ratio that determines the monopolisation of wealth by a global elite. Returns to the holders of capital (r) remain higher than the rate of return to economic growth (g), acting as a proxy for labour income, resulting in a growing inequality becoming embedded within the global 1% in relation to wider populations (Piketty, 2014, pp. 304–376).

Neither the work of Wilkinson and Pickett nor that of Piketty was new in and of itself, but instead was built upon a growing body of literature examining the impact of income inequality originating from both an academic and a non-academic resource base. Yet the two volumes brought academic rigour to an increasingly recognised social question and importantly demonstrated the structural nature of these phenomena which had become subject to wider social discourse. Thus, for example, the Black Report published in 1980 into health inequalities and the subsequent Health Divide Report in 1987 together outlined the extensive and persistent health inequalities within the UK (Townsend, Davidson and Whitehead 1982). Similarly, and more recently, Allyson Pollock (2004) continued this work examining relationships between health inequalities and social policy, while Antony Atkinson (1975 and 2015) had long been associated with the examination of income inequality. What was however novel about the work of Wilkinson and Pickett and Piketty, respectively, was the linkages drawn between income inequality and wider social questions, of health and social well-being, first in the case of *The Spirit Level* and second with long-run economic development in the case of *Capital in the Twenty-First Century*. Similarly, they pointed to issues of social and economic policy in mitigating and reversing the effects of these phenomena.

This new recognition and interest in inequality and the context in which the debate over income inequality arose was itself underpinned by the profound impact of the aftermath of the 2007 Great Financial Crash and the acceptance by governments that the financial sector, despite its creation of the crisis, was 'Too Big To Fail' (Tooze, 2019). The description of a banking and financial sector capable of holding governments' to ransom, through the bailing-out of a destructive and out of control financial sector, while making millions impoverished, shone a new light on the activities of the ruling elites in modern society (Lapavitsas et al., 2012; Varoufakis, 2017).

The debt-induced market for financialised Collateralised Debt Obligations, imploding in 2008, was responsible for sending the world's economies into the greatest economic collapse since the 1930s. The price to pay for this was a decade of austerity, resulting in the wider populations facing a generation of austerity, in order to resolve the crisis. However, the financial crisis also then shifted attention to the actions at the very top of society (Roberts, 2016). Thus, a focus which moved from the 'problem' of poverty into a 'problem' of inequality caused by the wealthiest in society's undue influence was met with the rapid development of an academic literature which had already began to develop and had deep roots in an established literature (Mazzucato, 2013; Dorling, 2014).

A more specific consideration of the inter-relationships between the dynamics of growth, inequality and well-being developed within the field of economics.

In an important contribution, Christop Lakner and Blanco Milanovic (2016, pp. 203–232; Milanovic, 2018) examined changes in the global income distribution since the 1990s demonstrating the emergence of an 'elephant curve' of income shares whereby the rise in income was located in the income deciles immediately above the lowest incomes, leading to the creation of a global 'middle' class, while those populations in the advanced economies saw stagnating or falling incomes. The elephant's trunk was then represented by the very top of the global income distribution which benefitted from soaring incomes for the wealthiest 1% of the global population. Lakner and Milanovic's analysis, while presented as an alternative to the evidence of Piketty, is, in reality, largely consistent with Piketty's evidence. Lakner and Milanovic (2016) identify the rising incomes of urbanisation and a newly emergent global working class, particularly within the newly industrialising economy of China and still more recently that of India. This focus upon developing rather than advanced economies, as focused upon by Piketty's (2014) study, facilitates a synthesis of approaches rather than alternative explanations. Alvaredo, Chancel, Piketty, Saez and Zucman's (2017 and 2018) work, updating that of Milanovic, similarly reaffirms this rapid rise in income inequality. They document the income stagnation for the majority of the world's populations occurring at the same time as a continued concentration of wealth among the very wealthiest elite (2017, Figure 2). Thus, Lakner, MIlanovic and Piketty can be understood as reinforcing one another. An understanding of broader economic changes in the wider global developments within late-twentieth-century capitalism.

A broad critique of these analyses comes from neo-classical economics as depicted by historian Deidre McCloskey (2017), whose interpretation of the evidence from the elephant curve is to suggest that it demonstrates the process of the continuing importance of the 'Great Enrichment'. McCloskey maintains that the process of capitalist development itself generates initial inequalities, yet over time greater equality emerges as a result of market forces. Trickle-down economics and Schumpeterian forms of creative destruction are the means by which greater equality is re-established and first-mover advantages competed away. McCloskey's central hypothesis is that it is the size of the 'cake' not its distribution that is of utmost importance. In a world of free markets and rationality, economic convergence is suggested to be an inevitable process. A normative approach to capitalist development is the model adopted in which a singular form of economic liberal, market-led capitalist development is the ideal and inequalities, poverty and the destruction of human lives are all a necessary cost in the transition from under-development to advanced capitalism. This model of economic development is rooted in a historically deterministic, or 'stages', approach to development which suggests an inevitable rise of poverty and inequality occurs following industrialisation, as characterised by Walt Whitman Rostow (1960), writing in the aftermath of the Second World War, identified five necessary stages in the 'take-off' to industrial development. It was only in the last 'maturity' phase where poverty and inequality could eventually be addressed by the development of a welfare state (Rostow, 1960, p. 74).

Social policy choices to address poverty and inequality would, within this framework, hinder or set back the development of the productive sector due to the opportunity costs of social policy. A crowding-out occurs where re-distribution or other investment in human capital is counter-posed and detrimental to the immediate private, market-driven accumulation of profit. Thus, within economics a widely recognised Kuznets inverted 'U'-shaped curve is suggested to explain the initial rise in poverty and inequality arising from industrialisation which later reduces as economies move beyond their initial industrial revolution (Krugman et al., 2012). Yet, even within these forms of explanation, specific policy choices can be identified which increase or reduce any nationally specific level of poverty and inequality. Most notably, literacy and health policy provide positive externalities to investment. A lack of access to clean drinking water for as many as one in nine of the world's population living in the most under-developed parts of the world impedes rather than accelerates the development of human capital (Wateraid, 2019). Similarly, the hundreds of textile factory workers in Dhaka, Bangladesh, making garments for multi-national European fashion stores in May 2013 died because of inadequate building construction brought on by an inequality of capitalist relationships between dominant fashion retailers and supply companies, not by inevitable laws of economic development (Chao, 2013). Thus, the Kuznet's curve, just as Malthus's law, cannot be understood as a natural law in which those living in a period of rapid industrialisation pay an intergenerational price for the increased wealth of the future population. What McCloskey and others ignore is the active role of government in enforcing redistribution as a means to development and the potential for limiting the extent to which market forces create negative externalities within the economy.

While neo-classical economics ignores distributional issues, under the guise of marginal rates of return, those engaged with inequality consider the development of growing inequality of major political and economic importance. The work of Alvaredo et al. (2017, 2018) and the World Inequality Lab has continued to identify the extent to which Lakner and Milanovic's elephant curve remains an accurate representation of the developmental path of income distribution for the richest 1% in society. While the features of the elephant curve can still be viewed, the extent of catch-up by the poorest is considerably lower than previously identified, yet the growth of wealth within the wealthiest 1% has increased relentlessly since 2008.

Poverty

While income inequality and wealth need to be fully represented in studies of poverty, the goal of such knowledge is to develop policy which addresses the needs of those who suffer as a result of this inequality, namely the poorest in society. Poverty and research into the causes of low-income households has a long tradition within the development of UK social policy. From the formation of the Elizabethan Poor Laws through to the development of the nascent welfare state with the Lloyd George reforms of 1906, to the Beveridge Report of 1937 and through to contemporary social policy, there has always been a tension between a welfare state providing limited support for the deserving poor in contrast to the construction of a universal system of social security in which all citizens have rights (Beveridge, 1942; Fraser, 1989).

Within the academic field, a wide range of studies have emerged. Peter Townsend's (1979) *Poverty in the United Kingdom* began a long-standing body of work in this area, documenting the extensive areas in which poverty could be identified and subsequently extended into official studies documenting deprivation within the UK (Townsend, Davidson and Whitehead, 1982). Similarly, John Hills (2004) examined the role of social security in its relief of poverty. Within the area of policy development and campaigning for policy change has seen a wide variety of non-governmental third-sector organisations emerge, including among others the Child Poverty Action Group, the Joseph Rowntree Foundation, Age UK examining pensioner poverty and Shelter addressing housing poverty at the national level but also at the transnational level the European Anti-Poverty Network or Save the Children, among many others.

Social exclusion

Income poverty is not, of course, the only means by which poverty and its alleviation is to be understood. Alternative measures and assessments of poverty began to emerge with the recognition that wider structural impediments to mobility might also be interacting with income poverty. Social exclusion and lack of access to resources which promote human capital formation became increasingly identified with means by which inequality and poverty were being reproduced (Hills and Stewart, 2005). Robert Puttman's (2000) ideas of social capital played an important role in these developments. The ability to engage in wider social environments was not understood to be solely linked to income but now identified as the inability to engage and interact with a series of wider social institutions. The hollowing out of the welfare state and undermining of wider forms of welfare provision impacted disproportionately on those social groups which were heavily reliant upon collective provision and without the necessary financial independence for access to private provision of services. Thus, the lack of public transport, closure of public libraries and reduction of childcare and educational facilities for early years' education all acted as indicators of wider deprivation and poverty. Together they also ensured those households suffering social exclusion faced increased barriers to their own ability to escape poverty or inequality (Bourdieu and Wacquant, 1992).

Here again we can identify two distinct approaches in which deficiency, as social exclusion, is identified. Pierre Bourdieu (1997), developed from a Marxist perspective, provides a focus upon the role of agency for users of social provision. Praxis, the ability to consciously engage and influence outcomes of welfare free from a pre-determined set of choices, is essential within the concept of agency as embedded within Bourdieu's framework. Social exclusion within this framework examines institutional barriers to inclusion for disadvantaged, minority or non-conformist populations. Barriers, as discrimination, are recognised as a means of social exclusion by states and institutions and remedies for discrimination linking policy outcomes such as universality, positive discrimination and equality of outcomes are the emphasis of policy formation within this framework.

In contrast, developed within a neo-classical supply-side approach, a framework focusing upon human capital formation linked to Puttman's understanding of social capital also emerged. Here, responses to social inclusion focused upon conformity and compliance as a precondition for welfare support as equality of opportunity provided a means to resolve inequalities. Social policy solutions which place an emphasis upon individual responsibility, conditionality on support and sanctions for non-compliance acted as the means by which behaviour could be nudged.

Happiness and human development

The focus upon a wider notion of poverty and inequality linked to non-income aspects of the lived experience also led to a broader development of poverty in terms of an understanding of human development and happiness. Within the advanced economies, happiness and its non-linear relationship with income has been a feature of work from Oswald (1997, pp. 1815–1831) and Layard (2005). Happiness, as this work suggests, has an 'n'-shaped relationship with household income such that initially happiness can be seen to rise with income but has declining marginal benefit beyond an optimal level and subsequently declines with rising income. This non-linearity leads to an identification of a cognitive dissonance between inequality and well-being and policy solutions which emphasise the role of positive psychology for the individual. Cognitive behavioural therapies or mindfulness approaches seek to increase the individual's recognition and acceptance of their social position, whether this be advantaged or disadvantaged.

Within a development context, the creation of a rights-based approach, primarily associated with the work of Sen (1985, 2009), and the creation of the United Nations Human Development Index have together provided a mechanism to explain the non-monetary aspects of cross-national relative social exclusion approaches to poverty. As the United Nations Development Programme maintains '*Human rights are the bedrock of human development. Human rights offer a useful perspective for analysing human development. Duty holders support and enhance human development and are accountable for a social system's failures to deliver human development*' (2016, p. 8). These perspectives not only go beyond the minimal claims of human development, but can also serve as a powerful tool in seeking remedies. UN Human Development Reports have then been instrumental in the creation and monitoring of a wider set of development goals identifying gender-based inequalities and educational and health inequalities together forming a multi-dimensional poverty index.

Cohort studies

Quantitative studies on poverty and inequality rely upon datasets which provide a snapshot of the levels of poverty at a specific point in time. While this provides researchers and policymakers with a picture of the prevalence of poverty and changes of the levels over time, what is absent is the extent to which the experience of poverty can be tracked across time. In order to assess the experience of poverty, qualitative research methods have typically been utilised to highlight the complexity of the 'lived experience'. Detailed and nuanced individual experience from qualitative research then replaces the representative evidence of the quantitative aggregate of individuals. Thus, there is little opportunity to develop a longer-term quantitative analysis of the experience of poverty and inequality using large datasets. Here, the household longitudinal panel study survey approach has a unique advantage. Household longitudinal panel surveys seek to not simply survey households to gain a quantitative dataset which is a snapshot at one specific point in time but seek to re-interview the same households in subsequent years in order to trace the changes in household circumstances over time. In household longitudinal panel studies, we have large quantitative data and in addition can draw inferences from the episodic re-interviewing of the household members across time.

The unit of analysis being adopted in this study is one of the households. Households are reconstituted from the individual data within the United Kingdom Household Longitudinal Panel Study (UKHLS) dataset in order to demonstrate the structural nature of inequality and poverty. As far back as the 1930s, William Beveridge (1942) identified a lifecycle of poverty arising from households' economic struggles to raise a family, through to ill health and old age. More recent work had utilised the concept of a propensity to poverty in recognition that not all households with the same characteristics will be in poverty.

A range of research papers on poverty and income inequality-related work made extensive use of the Understanding Society (UKHLS) predecessor dataset, the British Household Panel Survey, including an edited volume focused upon Scotland (Ermisch and Wright, 2005). However, more limited work on poverty and income inequality has been produced using the UKHLS dataset to date. Research on earlier years of the UKHLS dataset utilised single years of the data (Barnes et al., 2012) to examine poverty, while more recent publications, notably the Social Metric Foundation report (2020), made limited use of the longitudinal aspects of the dataset focusing only upon persistent poverty. The work of Hick and Lanau (2018) has utilised the longitudinal aspects to conclude that in-work poverty is a more transitory effect than for workless households but that the in-work poor has a higher propensity for moving into unemployment.

This work builds upon these earlier studies and extends the focus into an assessment of the potential for policy initiatives which alter the impact of poverty on specific household types. The following chapters in this volume provide, in Chapter 2, detail of the Understanding Society: United Kingdom Household Longitudinal Study survey. The chapter highlights the panel's data collection, sample selection and periodisation and in addition provides a basic introduction on statistics and the development of the derived income variable used throughout this study, namely equivalised real monthly household income after housing costs.

In Chapters 3 and 4, the study identifies the household characteristics of those at the bottom and top of the income distribution. Chapter 3 demonstrates the extent of structural poverty for those in the lowest income decile, while Chapter 4 repeats this analysis for those at the top of the income distribution. These two chapters then also quantify the extent of mobility into and out of these income deciles and in doing so highlight the limited nature of mobility for many of the poorest and richest households in the income distribution.

Chapters 5 and 6 use the UKHLS to examine the potential for redistribution policies and mechanisms for policy implementation. Chapter 5 examines the role of devolution and localisation of anti-poverty initiatives by highlighting the extent of variations in inequality across the UK nations and regions. The chapter uses Gini coefficients as a measure of inequality and concludes that devolution can be identified with a reduction of inequality relative to other regions of the UK. Chapter 6 again uses the measure of the Gini coefficient to identify anti-poverty strategies focused upon child poverty. Here, the focus is on policy design. The advantages and disadvantages of universal verses means-testing for targeted benefits are addressed and use the case study of free school meals. Universal provision both lowers inequality relative to the restricted means-testing system currently in place and also addresses the non-monetary barriers to welfare provision, namely stigma and non-take-up of benefits.

Chapter 7 in conclusion highlights the advantages of longitudinal research for policy development and the provision of an evidence base for policy evaluation. In this sense, this volume is not simply yet another contribution to a diverse and extensive literature on poverty and inequality. Instead, we hope it provides a future research agenda and introduction to a contemporary dataset to facilitate the examination of the extent and nature of household poverty and wealth within the UK. Our aim of this volume is that it goes beyond the simple documentation of contemporary poverty and inequality and encourages the utilisation of a newer and less-utilised longitudinal resource for the examination of these issues.

References

Alvaredo, F., Chancel, L., Piketty, T., Saez, E. and Zucman, G. (2017). The elephant curve of global inequality and growth, *Working Paper,* World Inequality Lab, available at https://eml.berkeley.edu/~saez/ACPSZ2018WIDWP.pdf accessed 3rd June 2018.

Alvaredo, F., Chancel, L., Piketty, T., Saez, E. and Zucman, G. (2018). World Inequality Report 2018, *World Inequality Lab*, available at http://wir2018.wid.world/files/download/wir2018-full-report-english.pdf

Atkinson, A. B. (1975), *The Economics of Inequality*, Oxford: Clarendon Press.

Atkinson, A. B. (2015), *Inequality: What Can Be Done?* Harvard, MA: Harvard University Press.

Barnes, M., Brown, A., Morrell, G., Rahim, N., Ross, A., Sadro, F. and Tipping, S. (2012), *Multi-Dimensional Poverty: A Research Methodology to Create Poverty Typologies*, London: NatCen Social Research.

BBC. (2021). https://www.bbc.co.uk/news/uk-41487126 accessed 10th November 2021.

Beveridge, W.H. (1942), *Social Insurance and Allied Services*, London: HMSO.

Bourdieu, P. (1997), *Outline of a Theory of Practice*. Cambridge: Cambridge University Press.

Bourdieu, P. and Wacquant, L. (1992), *An Invitation to Reflexive Sociology*, Chicago: University of Chicago Press.

Chao, R. (2013, June 16), Dhaka factory collapse: How far can businesses be held responsible? *Guardian*, available at https://www.theguardian.com/sustainable-business/dhaka-factory-collapse-businesses-held-responsible accessed 20th June 2018.

Colbeck, R. (ed.) (2010, October 8). The Income parade, Personal Blog, available at https://learn1.open.ac.uk/mod/oublog/viewpost.php?post=24245 accessed 21st May 2018.

Dorling, D. (2014), *Inequality and the 1%*, London: Verso.

Engels, F. (1996, February 6), Outlines of a Critique of Political Economy, *Collected Works*. Transcribed for the Internet by director@marx,org, available at http://mysite.du.edu/~rkuhn/ints4465/engels.pdf accessed 3rd June 2018.

Ermisch, J.F. and Wright, R.E. (2005), *Changing Scotland: Evidence from the British Household Panel Survey*, Bristol: Policy Press.

Fawcett Society. (2020), *Equal Pay Day*, available at https://www.fawcettsociety.org.uk/news/the-fawcett-society-announces-date-of-equal-pay-day-2020 accessed 2nd May 2021.

Financial Times. (2018), Javid marks home secretary debut by rejecting May's 'hostile environment', 1st May, p. 1.

Financial Times. (2021). https://www.ft.com/content/b02f1e93-3e63-4881-a053-4e46d8e12208 accessed 10th November 2021.

Flannery K. and Marcus J. (2012), *The Creation of Inequality: How Our Prehistoric Ancestors Set the Stage for Monarchy, Slavery and Empire*. Cambridge, MA: Harvard University Press.

Fraser, D. (1989), *Evolution of the British Welfare State: A History of Social Policy Since the Industrial Revolution* (2nd edition), Basingstoke, Hampshire: MacMIllan.

Guardian. (2018), PM forced to crack down on 'dirty money', 2nd May, pp. 1 and 4.

Guardian. (2021), https://www.theguardian.com/commentisfree/2021/nov/09/tory-sleaze-british-politics-labour-scandals accessed 10th November 2021.

Herald. (2018), Day of reckoning for alcohol policy, 2nd May, p. 1.

Hick, R. and Lanau, A. (2018), Moving In and Out of In-Work Poverty in the UK: An Analysis of Transitions, Trajectories and Trigger Events. *Journal of Social Policy* 47(4), October 2018, pp. 661–682.

Hills, J. (2004), *Inequality and the State*, Oxford: Oxford University Press.

Hills, J. and Stewart, K. (eds.) (2005), *A More Equal Society: New Labour, Poverty, Inequality and Exclusion*, Bristol: The Policy Press.

Knies, G. (2017), *Understanding Society: The UK Household Longitudinal Study Waves 1–7 User Guide*, Colchester: University of Essex, Institute for Social and Economic Research.

Krugman, P.R., Obstfeld, M. and Melitz, M.J. (2012), *International Economics: Theory and Policy*, Pearson: London.

Lakner, C. and Milanovic, B. (2016). Global Income Distribution: From the Fall of the Berlin Wall to the Great Recession. *The World Bank Economic Review* 30(2), pp. 203–232.

Lapavitsas, C., Kaltenbrunner, A., Labrinidis, G., Lindo, D., Meadway, J., Mitchell, J., Painceira, J.P., Pires, E., Powell, J., Stenfors, A., Teles, N. and Vatikiotis, L.(eds.) (2012), *Crisis in the Eurozone*, London: Verso.

Layard, R. (2005*). Happiness: Lessons from a New Science*. London: Penguin Books.
Malthus, T. (1964), 'A Summary View of the Principle of Population', in F.W. Notestein (ed.), *Three Essays on Population*, New York: Mentor Books.
Mazzucato, M. (2013), *The Entrepreneurial State: Debunking Public vs Private Sector Myths*, London: Penguin.
McCloskey, D.N. (2017), Measured, Unmeasured, Mismeasured, and Unjustified Pessimism: A Review Essay of Thomas Piketty's Capital in the Twenty-First Century, *Erasmus Journal of Philosophy and Economics*, available at http://www.deirdremccloskey.org/docs/pdf/PikettyReviewEssay.pdf accessed 3rd February 2018.
Meek, R.L. (1953), *Marx and Engles on Malthus*, London: Lawrence and Wishart.
Milanovic, B. (2018), *Global Inequality: A New Approach for the Age of Globalization*, Cambridge, MA: Harvard University Press.
O'Brien, O. (2014), *Lives on the Line: A Map of Life Expectancy at Birth*, available at http://oobrien.com/2014/10/tube-tongues/ accessed 3rd July 2018.
Oswald, A. (1997), Happiness and Economic Performance. *Economic Journal* 107(445), pp. 1815–1831.
Pen, J. (1974), *Income Distribution*, London: Pelican Books.
Piketty, T. (2014), Capital in the Twenty-First Century, Cambridge, MA: Harvard University Press.
Pollock, A. (2004), *NHS Plc: The Privatisation of Our Health Care*, London: Verso.
Puttman, R.D. (2000), *Bowling Alone: The Collapse and Revival of American Community*, New York: Simon and Schuster.
Roberts, M. (2016), *The Long Depression: How It Happened, Why It Happened and What Happens Next*, Chicago: Haymarket.
Rostow, W.W. (1960), *The Stages of Economic Growth: A non-Communist Manifesto*, Cambridge: Cambridge University Press.
Sen, A. (1985), Well-Being, Agency and Freedom: The Dewey Lectures 1984. *Journal of Philosophy* 2(4), pp. 169–221.
Sen, A. (2009), *The Idea of Justice*, Cambridge, MA: Harvard University Press.
Social Metrics Foundation. (2020), *Measuring Poverty 2020: A Report of the Social Metrics Foundation*, London: Legatum Institute.
Tooze, A. (2019), *Crashed: How a Decade of Financial Crises Changed the World*, London: Penguin.
Townsend, P. (1979), *Poverty in the United Kingdom*, London: Allen Lane and Penguin Books.
Townsend, P., Davidson, N. and Whitehad, M. (1982), *Inequalities in Health: The Black Report and the Health Divide*, Harmondsworth Middx: Penguin.
United Nations Development Programme. (2016), *Human Development Report: Human Development for Everyone*, New York: United Nations, available at http://hdr.undp.org/sites/default/files/2016_human_development_report.pdf accessed 20th March 2018.
Varoufakis, Y. (2017), *Adults in the Room: My Battle with Europe's Deep Establishment*, London: Penguin.
Wateraid. (2019), https://www.wateraid.org/uk/water accessed 3rd May 2019.
Wilkinson, R. and Pickett, K. (2009), *The Spirit Level: Why More Equal Societies Almost Always Do Better*, London: Penguin Books.
Wilkinson, R. and Pickett, K. (2019), *The Inner Level: How More Equal Societies Reduce Stress, Restore Sanity and Improve Everyone's Well-being*, London: Penguin Books.

2

UNDERSTANDING SOCIETY

Subjectivity, datasets and methodological approaches

Introduction

This chapter introduces the UK Household Longitudinal Study (UKHLS) survey, Understanding Society, used throughout this book. We assume no knowledge of either the data or statistics of our readers, and this chapter builds the step-by-step methodological approach adopted to examining the dataset and some basic statistical concepts used throughout the book. If the reader is familiar with longitudinal datasets and data analysis, then they may choose to skip this chapter. However, for those for whom data and its analysis is new, we seek to demonstrate that with the use of a few concepts, large datasets can provide deep insights into the experience of poverty and inequality in our society.

But what concepts do we wish to adopt? All quantitative evidence is subject to bias and subjectivity from both the organisations gathering the data and the subjectivity of the researcher examining the data. What evidence is to be quantified? Which questions are to be asked? Of whom are they asked and how are the responses recorded? All of the answers to these questions are subjective, and in their answers lie deeply political, social and ideological assumptions. Thus, while quantitative analysis may be presented as 'objective' due to the lack of bias within the individual elements of the data, the choice of which data to extract and the methods used to represent the data are highly subjective (Lazer, Kennedy, King and Vespignani, 2014).

In contrast, qualitative data allows for the richness of the human experience to be presented, often through the voice of the subjects of the research (Solesbury, 2002). Certainly, many qualitative studies of the lived experience facilities and gives richness to quantitative evidence (Martin, 2001). However, individuals and populations are not identical and the representativeness of the individual lived experience can too often be dismissed in social policy formation for its unrepresentativeness.

DOI: 10.4324/9781315179957-2

Our starting point is, however, different. We seek to demonstrate that quantitative evidence available through large-scale household datasets, such as the UKHLS, provide representative evidence that informs and is reinforced by the messages derived from more qualitative studies. We seek to allow the data to give voice to the lived experience of poverty and inequality facing households in contemporary British society, and demonstrate the validity of using quantitative research in the development of social policy linked to poverty and inequality.

For this to take place, we need to first and foremost be explicit about our own subjectivities in this study.

The first is income. Our view is that while money (or income) will never be the sole determinant of happiness in life, it can certainly help to improve it whether directly (e.g. through being able to purchase a better lifestyle) or indirectly (e.g. through offering peace of mind in uncertain times) money has the potential to relieve hardship, and therefore it must be of crucial importance to any examination of the human condition. Other factors will be important (e.g. love and friendship, the arts and social inclusion etc), but money and what flows from it will always be significant. Our analysis, therefore, begins by placing money (income) centre-stage.

The second is the household. Contemporary capitalist society is not simply the aggregation of a society of individuals. Within the social sciences, we are familiar with the way in which different individual characteristics intersect with one another. While class, gender, race and disability are easily recognised areas of research, researchers also recognise that the intersection between different characteristics plays an important part in identifying variation across the subjects at the centre of a study. Intersectionality may therefore be helpful for the examination of individuals experience within a society; however, at the same time, it does so to the exclusion of the recognition that individual's interaction within society is not one at the level of the individual. Instead individuals combine together to form family and household units. These units may be made up of just a single individual, individuals who have no relationship with one another or as a multi-generational family unit. Whatever forms these households take, they nevertheless form collective social households. In capturing the intersections between distinct individuals within a household unit, we therefore have an opportunity to examine a collective rather than an individual experience of poverty and inequality. Households are neither homogenous in form nor free from inequalities internally, but they are the structures through which social interaction is constituted. Therefore, when considering issues of poverty, it is necessary to understand that households may reflect more than a single characteristic, and the experience of poverty and inequality may impact individuals who themselves do not have a specific characteristic. Thus, for example, child poverty is not simply the poverty of children but of the whole household.

Finally, before examining our conceptual approach to analysing the dataset, it is necessary to say something about the authors' own preferences and subjectivities. The authors of this book have for many years engaged in examining poverty and inequality from a social science and policy-focused perspective. We seek to not simply identify the extent of poverty or inequality through the use of longitudinal data, but seek to identify policy measures and quantify their impact on the alleviation of poverty and inequality. We thus identify ourselves with the research itself and do not wish to identify as objective by-sanders in this process. We hold diametrically opposed political and social viewpoints but nevertheless reject the suggestion that choice of data, the choice of measures to examine data and the representation of results of data analysis are in some way objective. It is to the choice of measures that we now turn to be explicit to the reader of our biases.

The UK household longitudinal study

The UKHLS, also known as the *Understanding Society* dataset, is the UK's largest and most information-rich panel dataset for the study of households and individuals living in the UK. Since 2009, the data has been collected through face-to-face interviews on behalf of the Institute for Social and Economic Research (ISER) at the University of Essex; over a period of many months, they process the raw data to generate a version of the data useful to researchers, to whom it is then made available for them to empirically analyse.

The UKHLS is not the first such household dataset that has been made available with public funding. The UKHLS's predecessor was the British Household Panel Survey (BHPS) that ran from 1991 to 2008. The BHPS's sample size was 5,511 households containing 10,263 individuals in 1991 and had expanded to 8,114 households containing 14,419 individuals by 2008. However, after consultations with key BHPS dataset users, the decision was taken to significantly enhance the dataset that was offered to researchers in both scale and scope of issues addressed, with the result being the UKHLS dataset starting in 2009 with a significantly increased sample size, see **Table 2.1**.

Therefore, the sample size of the UKHLS is around three to four times that of the BHPS, permitting a more meaningful analysis of groups and sub-groups within society that are quite small in percentage terms. A large initial sample size is particularly important for analysis, such as undertaken throughout this book,

TABLE 2.1 UK Household Longitudinal Study Summary Information

Wave	*Data Collection Period*	*Total Number of Households*	*Adults*
(A)	2009–2010	30,169	50,993
(B)	2010–2011	30,508	54,597
(C)	2011–2012	27,782	49,739
(D)	2012–2013	25,875	47,157
(E)	2013–2014	24,369	44,903
(F)	2014–2015	24,516	45,289
(G)	2015–2016	23,063	42,217

Source: Waves A–G of the UKHLS (2010–2016).

which seeks to sub-divide the data by different household characteristics. Sub-division of the data by income, household type and geography will result in a rapid loss of representativeness without a large initial sample.

Whereas the annual panel data for the BHPS was collected primarily in the September of each year, with the following months used to collect missing data of households that had moved since their last interview or household members that were absent when interviewers went to their homes, the design of the UKHLS was such that data was collected over a somewhat longer time period. However, these phases of data collection were themselves not overlapping and we can identify each wave of the data with a specific time period. For consistency we utilise the end date for the time frame with respect to identifying each wave, thus while Wave A covers 2009–2010 we refer to it as 2010 and so on.

The panel nature of the UKHLS

The intended *panel* nature of the UKHLS dataset means that to the greatest extent possible the ISER attempts to track the same sample of households and individuals through time. This enables researchers to look not only at the characteristics of the UKHLS at a specific point in time, or even at a series of points in time, but to also track the changes in circumstances of particular households and individuals over time. This time dimension enables researchers to distinguish between related but different concepts such as (a) a household *being* poor, (b) a household *becoming* poor and (c) a household *remaining* poor – although these circumstances are likely to be related, they are different and the consequences (and policy imperatives) can differ significantly (an individual being poor for one week may be less of a concern (to them and policymakers) than that individual being poor for a decade).

The data in **Table 2.1** clearly indicates that the UKHLS sample size has not remained constant over time. The data contained in household panel datasets change in composition for two main reasons. First, interviewing all members of the dataset is not always possible and although the individuals remain in the dataset itself, they may not be interviewed on every occasion.

Although the UKHLS is funded by the government, participation in it is voluntary; some household members may be temporarily unavailable, or simply refuse to participate even if other household members choose to do so. Thus, a comparison of **Tables 2.1** and **2.2** shows that of the 50,993 adults included in the sample of households in **Table 2.1**, only 47,732 of them (93.6%) are fully interviewed in Wave A shown in **Table 2.2**. Very basic information about the other 6.4% of adults in those households will be obtained by questions to those household members who do participate. A second area of the variation arises from the expected inevitability of deaths, household composition changes and household geographical mobility. In **Table 2.2**, we see a more complete picture of the extent to which the UKHLS dataset has retained its original sample, and therefore permits researchers to track them through time.

TABLE 2.2 UKHLS Wave A Sample Retention

Wave	*Wave A Interviewed Adults*	*Wave on Wave Retention Percentage*
A	47,732	
B	35,488	74.35%
C	28,643	80.71%
D	24,800	86.58%
E	22,280	89.84%
F	19,176	86.07%
G	17,133	89.35%

Source: Waves A (2010)–G (2016) of the UKHLS.

Thus, of the 47,732 adults fully interviewed in Wave A, 35,488 of them (74.35%) were also fully interviewed in Wave B; of these, 28,643 (80.71% of 35,488) were also interviewed in Wave C, and so on (thus, 28,643 adults were interviewed in Wave A, Wave B and Wave C, and 17,133 adults were interviewed in each of the seven waves). **Table 2.2** suggests that retention from one wave to the next increased from about 75% at the start of the panel to almost 90% at the end of the panel – this pattern of increasing wave-on-wave retention is common in panel datasets.

Another aspect of the design of the UKHLS apparent from **Tables 2.1** and **2.2** is that there is some replenishment of the sample with new households and individuals in an attempt to offset the loss of existing sample members (i.e. the attrition in the sample). **Table 2.1** shows that the sample at Wave G, 42,217 adults, though not quite enough to maintain the original sample size remains greater than the number of adults in **Table 2.2** who have been present at each wave subsequent to Wave A, 35,488 in Wave B and falling to 17,133 in Wave G respectively. This acquisition of new sample members is specifically selected in an attempt to maintain the representativeness of the sample (Jäckle, Gaia, Al Baghal, Burton and Lynn, 2017).

The advantages of panel data over forms of longitudinal data

Panel data such as the UKHLS is just one example of longitudinal data (i.e. data that encompasses a time element). Other types include cohort datasets (where researchers follow a defined group through time without any replenishment when attrition occurs) and retrospective studies (where researchers ask respondents about events in the past). Panel data has important (but different) advantages over both of these alternative data formats.

When forming a cohort, it is often the case that it starts as a non-representative sample of the population, and there is no acquisition of new members to rectify that problem later on; this is particularly the case when considering a birth cohort such as the National Child Development Study (NCDS) cohort of 17,000 children born in Great Britain (i.e. England, Scotland and Wales) during a single week of 1958. Even where the original sample begins as representative of the population as a whole, the ageing (and dying) process ensures that it becomes increasingly old and therefore non-representative. To the extent that the increasingly non-representative sample has differing personal characteristics and behaviours compared to society as a whole, analysis of them risks offering only an increasingly misleading set of results.

For retrospective studies, the main disadvantage is recall bias – a situation whereby people forget certain events (e.g. short spells of unemployment in between jobs), or information relating to those events (e.g. the start and finish dates of events, or job attributes such as pay rates). There is also the potential for respondents to base recollections of the past on the basis of how they feel about the present. In contrast, the UKHLS asks respondents about their 'current' income, health and so forth.

The age distribution of the UKHLS

The age distribution of the adult respondents in the UKHLS (as of Wave A) is illustrated in **Figure 2.1**. The data suggests that the survey design has been relatively successful in encompassing a broad sweep of the United Kingdom population in terms of age, with only a few small outliers – the survey seems to be picking up smaller numbers of the very youngest adults (16- & 17-year-olds), has a slight over-representation of individuals in their mid-40s (potentially reflecting the housing and geographical stability of those with families) and does seem to be picking up the effect of the generation born just after the second world war (who would be in their early-60s at that point in time).

All of these individuals would have been identified as living in households sampled by the UKHLS, and every effort would have been made to fully

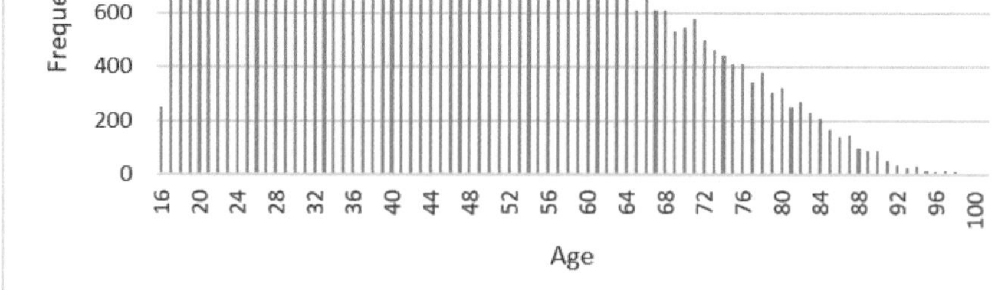

FIGURE 2.1 Age distribution of adults in the UKHLS (Wave A)

TABLE 2.3 UKHLS Household Composition (Percentages)

Wave	*A*	*B*	*C*	*D*	*E*	*Mean A to E*
Single occupant	25.16	24.99	25.18	26.86	27.15	25.79
In addition to head of household, the household has the following members:						
Partner	57.45	59.28	59.49	58.72	58.68	58.71
Other adult(s)	44.06	43.74	44.10	43.42	43.25	43.73
Children (0–15)	13.57	13.37	12.83	11.72	11.14	12.61
Children (0–1)	1.59	1.28	0.80	0.25	0.27	0.88
Children (2–4)	3.10	3.13	2.67	2.14	1.88	2.63
Children (5–7)	3.10	3.05	3.28	3.09	2.77	3.06
Children (8–10)	3.06	2.96	2.94	2.95	2.91	2.97
Children (11–12)	2.16	2.11	2.09	1.86	1.99	2.05
Children (13–15)	3.21	3.26	3.25	3.10	3.05	3.18
N	30,169	30,508	27,782	25,875	24,369	27,741

Source: UKHLS Waves A–E (2010–2014).

NB: 'Other adult(s)' would include the children of the Head of Household if they are 16 years or older.

NB: The 0–1 and 11–12 age ranges are of shorter duration than the others, and so would be expected to contain fewer children.

interview them. However, there is also the issue of children in the sample households (defined as being under the age of 16). Basic personal information (gender, age, relation to others in the household, etc.) would have been recorded for all children living in sample households. In addition, for children between the ages of 11 & 15 inclusive, a child-specific questionnaire was asked each year. Overtime, as these children aged to become young adults, they would subsequently be interviewed using the adult questionnaire.

The composition of households (in terms of adults & children) for Waves A–E is summarised in **Table 2.3**. Relevant to the purposes of this book, and explored in greater detail in Chapter 6, is the distribution of children by households. **Table 2.3** highlights, in the final column, that on average 12.61% of households currently contain children (conversely 87.39% of households do not contain children under the age of 16). The number of households with children might appear low but this represents merely a snapshot of household composition at a particular point in time – the children of some parents will no longer be under the age of 16 and will themselves be considered to be adults in the UKHLS, and some couples are yet to start the families that they will eventually have. Furthermore, the birth rate in the has declined in recent decades, such that the total fertility rate had fallen to 1.83 per woman by 2014 (Office for National Statistics, 2014) and is evidenced by the falling percentage of households in the UKHLS with a child aged between 0 and 1 years of age in **Table 2.3**.

A little over one-quarter of households (25.16% in wave A, 2010) contain only one occupant, while a little under 60% of households (57.45% in Wave A, 2010) contain a couple in a marital or cohabiting relationship. Over 40% of households (44.06% in Wave A, 2010) contain adults who are not in a marital or cohabiting relationship with the Head of Household; some, though not all, of these 'other' adults, will be their children. A little over 10% of households (13.57% in Wave A, 2010) contain children under the age of 16.

The above section provides a short descriptive introduction to the structure of the UKHLS. It is now necessary to introduce some basic statistical ideas in advance of their use in the following chapters.

Methodology

Averages

Datasets such as the UKHLS contain highly detailed information about the income and other characteristics of its sample of individuals and households in the UK, and investigating that information enables researchers to examine the extent and nature of inequality, wealth and poverty. However, making sense of that information requires its aggregation to ensure that those analyses are manageable and the results are informative; such aggregation/analysis typically yields average values as a way of representing, in a simple form, the most important results to be obtained from analysis of the detailed raw data. But what is meant by an average? and do they illuminate the most useful points or misleadingly conceal more important information?

There are many things that people may think of when using or hearing the word 'average', but here we wish to consider three specific statistical averages – the mean, the median and the mode. All are averages, yet rarely, are they going to provide the same result? We will explain their meaning using simple examples;

The mean

When the word 'average' is used the statistical concept that most people think of is the mean. It is simply the number that you obtain when you add up a series of numbers and divide by how many numbers you have. Thus, in example (2.1), the mean of the numbers 5 and 9 is 7:

$$mean = \frac{5+9}{2} = \frac{14}{2} = 7 \tag{2.1}$$

Its appeal as a measure of 'averageness' stems from the fact that it is intuitive, commonly used, relatively easy to calculate, and all of the numbers used in its calculation are considered of equal importance to the final average; furthermore, the resulting mean seems to be representative of the underlying series of numbers from which it is calculated. Another example (2.2) that illustrates these characteristics would be the mean of the following four numbers – 3, 5, 7 and 9:

$$mean = \frac{3+5+7+9}{4} = \frac{24}{4} = 6 \tag{2.2}$$

Both of the above examples calculate a series of numbers that are relatively close together and can be described as representative even though in example (2.2) the mean is not a number in the actual series used. However, if the series of numbers include some that are very different from the rest ('*outliers*') then, although the resulting mean may be calculated in a correct manner, it ceases to 'feel' representative. That is, it fails to reflect the data it is identifying. Calculating the mean for the following number series (5, 3, 10, 100 and 2) illustrates this:

$$mean = \frac{5+3+10+100+2}{5} = \frac{120}{5} = 24 \qquad (2.3)$$

While the mean has been correctly calculated as 24, it is a lot different from all of the numbers from which it has been calculated and, therefore, it is difficult to view it as being representative. This problem is greatest when the number series contains extreme outliers; in a world where the richest 1% have personal wealth that the other 99% can scarcely begin to imagine, using the mean to measure average income results in a value that represents the financial circumstances of almost no-one. The median, our second measure of 'averageness' attempts to address this problem.

The median

The median basically means the 'middle one' – if you order the numbers in a series from lowest to highest, the median is the one in the middle. Using the number series in example 2.3 above, we would first of all order the series into 2, 3, 5, 10 and 100, and then choose the middle one – that is, 5. Its 'averageness' steam from the fact that half of the other values (2 and 3) lie below it and the other half of the other values (10 & 100) lie above it. The median (5) seems more representative of this series of numbers than the mean (24). In a society with unequal income, the mean implies an 'average' standard of living beyond the reality of almost all of the people. For this reason, many researchers of income inequality prefer the median measure because it is not distorted by a small number of very rich people.

The mode

However, although the median measure avoids the distortion that outliers can cause for the mean measure, it is nonetheless the case that it does not always represent the best measure for indicating the typical value of something. Consider the following number series: 2, 2, 2, 10, 20, 30 and 39. The mean is 15 while the median is 10, but is either the mean or median 'typical'. Many people would look at that series and think that two (appearing three times) is more typical than ten (appearing only once). The mode of a number series reflects this 'most common' perspective on 'averageness', picking out the number that appears most often. Thus, the mode of the above number series is two.

BOX 2.1

ODD NUMBERS

Where there is an odd number of numbers in the series, there will always be a 'middle one'. But when there is an even number of numbers in the series, there is no 'middle one'. Consider the following number series: 5, 3, 10, 100, 2 and 12. When sorted low to high, this becomes 2, 3, 5, 10, 12 and 100. The median is calculated as the mean of the two middle numbers – that is, the mean of 5 and 10 (i.e. 7.5).

Mean, median or mode – Which is the best measure?

The most commonly used measure is the mean, though many researchers in the fields of inequality and poverty also like to make use of the median measure. The mode measure is infrequently used. Does this mean that the mean measure is the best? No, each measure has its own context-specific advantages and disadvantages and can add valuable insights into an analysis. In this book, we will use whichever measure(s) to shed most light on the issue that we are examining at that point.

The UKHLS and measures of income, income deciles and distributions

'Average' household income levels

The starting point for our analysis of household income is the total income (from all sources) that households gain in a month. Researchers who examine household finances sometimes choose to focus on that income that remains after a household has paid their income-related taxes (in the United Kingdom, such taxes would include Income Tax and Employee National Insurance Contributions), but we focus on income before deductions of income-related taxes. We refer to this as Gross Monthly Household Income (GMHI). In the first year, Wave A of the UKHLS dataset **Table 2.4** shows the mean, median, mode, minimum and maximum of this household income variable is:

TABLE 2.4 UKHLS Gross Monthly Household Income, Wave A (2010)

Mean	£2,909.47
Median	£2,249.84
Mode	£0.00
Minimum	–£13,373.08
Maximum	£20,000.00
Number of observations	30,169

Source: UKHLS Wave A (2010).

From **Table 2.4**, we can see that the first time this data was collected provided a total sample of observations of 30,169 different households. These households were recorded as having GMHI ranging from (negative) £13,373 up to (positive) £20,000. Both of these numbers need a little explanation.

First, some households would include one or more self-employed individuals whose income would include the profit or loss from their self-employment business. Where such losses exist and are greater than any positive incomes going to them and/or other members of their households, such households would be recorded as having a negative GMHI level. There are 44 such negative income households (0.15% of the UKHLS dataset in Wave A); for half of these households, their negative income is less than (negative) £1,000. The presence of such small numbers of negative income levels does not undermine the validity of the analyses presented in this book.

Second, some of our households include one or more individuals on very high incomes. Providing personal information to the UKHLS is not a legal requirement, and such individuals may well prefer to withhold such information, particularly if their incomes are very high. Therefore, to encourage such individuals to participate in the survey and provide income data, the publicly available versions of the UKHLS data has truncated versions of some income variables. In the case of the GMHI variable, this truncation occurs at £20,000 per month (all households with monthly incomes above £20,000 will have their income recorded as £20,000).[1] There are 116 households for whom there is a GMHI of £20,000 or more (0.38% of our sample). Although this truncation does mean that our data is less accurate for this top 0.38% of households, few of the analyses presented in this book will be significantly affected, though special care should be given when interpreting results in Chapter 4, focusing on those households at the top of the income distribution (where wealth rather than poverty is examined in more detail).

Table 2.4 also shows that the mean level of our GMHI variable is £2,909, compared to the median of £2,250. That the mean is higher than the median is a standard outcome when analysing income data, since as we have already noted there is the potential for high-income outliers to have a greater effect on the mean than the median. This tells us that the distribution of incomes across households itself is not a standard distribution but instead the peak of the distribution is shifted towards the lower end of the income distribution.

The mode income level is £0. At first sight, this might appear to indicate that no income at all is a common outcome for many households, in contrast to the more encouraging picture painted by the mean and median measures. However, 'unusual' results for the mode measure is actually quite common when dealing with what can be called a 'continuous' variable.[2] Only 319 households (1.06% of our sample) recorded £0 income; in contrast, most other GMHI values were recorded for only a very small number of households (often only one household). This illustrates that care needs to be taken in choosing the most appropriate statistical measure to capture the fundamental message contained in data. In the

TABLE 2.5 UKHLS Gross Monthly Household Income, 2010–2014

Wave	*A*	*B*	*C*	*D*	*E*	*Mean A to E*
Mean GMHI	£2,909	£3,098	£3,205	£3,281	£3,312	£3,161
Median GMHI	£2,250	£2,459	£2,571	£2,604	£2,612	£2,499
N	30,169	30,508	27,782	25,875	24,369	

Source: UKHLS Waves A–E (2010–2014).

case of our GMHI variable, the mean and median values are the most revealing, though we accept that the extreme outcomes captured by the mode are still of interest, and could represent extreme hardship for the households concerned.

The key advantage of the UKHLS dataset over other panel datasets is that we can follow our sample of households over time, and this longitudinal element of the data is utilised in **Table 2.5** which examines the mean and median GMHI values for each of the first five annual waves of UKHLS data from 2010 to 2014. **Table 2.5** shows that both the mean and the median values increase through the UKHLS period, with the mean GMHI increasing from £2,909 to £3,312, while the median income rises from £2,250 to £2,612 over the same five waves of data.

An increase in the mean level of GMHI of 13.85% in the four years, separating Waves A and E, might suggest a degree of rising prosperity after the financial crash of 2007–2008, but these years were seen by many politicians and commentators as a period when a 'cost of living crisis' afflicted many households (Emmerson and Joyce, 2014) – for many households, any rise in income levels were more than offset by rises in prices. Therefore, a more accurate picture of changes in household incomes over time would be provided by looking not at the nominal level of GMHI, but rather the real level of it (i.e. stripping out the effects of price inflation) – this can be achieved by deflating the nominal levels presented in **Table 2.5** by a relevant price index. Many price indices are published by the government's Office for National Statistics, but the price index, most relevant to household income, is the Retail Price Index (RPI) (Office for National Statistics, 2015). **Table 2.6** shows the annual percentage increase in the RPI over the period of our UKHLS data.

Thus, the basket of goods and services covered by the RPI was 5.6% more expensive in September 2011 than they were in September 2010. Using these price inflation values to deflate the nominal GMHI values in **Table 2.5**, we

TABLE 2.6 Percentage Increase in the Retail Prices Index

Month	*% Increase in RPI in preceding 12 months*	*Cumulative % increase in RPI*
September 2011	5.6%	5.6%
September 2012	2.6%	8.3%
September 2013	3.2%	11.8%
September 2014	0.8%	12.7%

Source: Office of National Statistics.

TABLE 2.7 ULHLS Real Gross Monthly Household Income 2010–2014

Wave	*A*	*B*	*C*	*D*	*E*	*Mean A to E*
Mean GMHI	£2,909	£2,934	£2,958	£2,934	£2,939	£2,935
Median GMHI	£2,250	£2,329	£2,373	£2,329	£2,318	£2,320
N	30,169	30,508	27,782	25,875	24,369	

Source: UKHLS Waves A–E (2010–2014).

obtain the real GMHI values in **Table 2.7**. The effect of the cost-of-living crisis is now apparent, with the mean of real GMHI rising from £2,909 to £2,939 per month (just 1.03%) over these five periods and a rise from £2,250 to £2,318 (3.02%) in the median real GMHI. Although these data do point to rising real GMHI values, it is certainly the case that for many households, the recovery from the 2007–2008 financial crash was as Dorling (2014) identifies was very limited, at best, and is explored in greater detail in Chapters 3 and 4. Throughout our study, all household income data reported will be real values at 2010 prices.

Earned, unearned and transfer income

One of the particularly useful features of the UKHLS is that it provides very detailed income information for its respondent households not just only the aggregate income level, but also its various sources (e.g. labour earnings, pensions, interest, dividends, etc.). This level of detail is useful not only because it allows for a more accurate picture of poverty and wealth to be developed, but also because it permits a more detailed analysis of policy options explored in Chapters 5 and 6. At this point, it is possible to summarise the UKHLS income data by classifying it in broad terms according to three mutually exclusive sources:

- Earned income (from current employment)
- Asset-based income (e.g. rent received, interest received, dividends)
- Welfare income (including, but not limited to, pensions [both private and public] and transfers from family members such as alimony and child maintenance)

The clear picture to emerge from **Table 2.8** is that the biggest contributor to real gross monthly household incomes (a mean of £2,214 per month across our five waves of data from 2010 to 2014) is earned income, contributing 75% of mean real GMHI; this compares to only £86, 3% of mean real GMHI, for asset-based income and £635, contributing 22% of mean GMHI, for welfare income.

Comparing like with like for households: Equivalence scales

Although some elements of household expenditure may in some circumstances be fixed in that they do not rise in line with household size (e.g. a couple may live in a one bedroom home, just like a single person might), for many other elements

TABLE 2.8 UKHLS Real Gross Monthly Household Income Disaggregated by Source 2010–2014

Wave	*A*	*B*	*C*	*D*	*E*	*Mean A to E*
Mean GMHI	£2,909	£2,934	£2,958	£2,934	£2,939	£2,935
Earned income	£2,293	£2,202	£2,215	£2,181	£2,178	£2,214
Asset-based income	£66	£76	£91	£98	£100	£86
Welfare income	£551	£655	£653	£655	£661	£635
N	30,169	30,508	27,782	25,875	24,369	

Source: UKHLS Waves A–E (2010–2014).

of household expenditure (e.g. food, clothing, energy, etc.) more household members incur more household expenditure. The consequence of this is that the standard of living a household can achieve from a given household income depends on the number and type of individual members within the household. Therefore, analyses of household incomes to investigate household poverty and inequality need to take account of household composition.

The standard way to achieve this is to apply a 'correction' to the real household income data to take account of the different composition of those households – that is, to use an "equivalence scale" to obtain equivalised measures of household income. One of the most common equivalence scales used in the poverty literature is the McClements Scale (De Vos and Asghar Zaidi, 1977). Each member of the household adds to the McClements Scale score on the basis of their age and their relationship to the head of household as per **Table 2.9**.

Thus, for example, a household containing only one person would have a McClements Scale score of 0.61, while adding a spouse would add 0.39 to the score (resulting in a score of 1). A different second adult (e.g. suppose the household contained only two friends sharing rather than cohabiting, scored as 0.46) would yield a score of 1.07 (i.e. 0.61 + 0.46). This different score (1.07 vs 1) reflects

TABLE 2.9 The McClements Scale

Household Member	*Contribution to McClements Scale*
Head of Household	0.61
Partner of Head of Household	0.39
Other second adult	0.46
Third adult	0.42
Other adult	0.39
Children (0–1 years)	0.09
Children (2–4 years)	0.18
Children (5–7 years)	0.21
Children (8–10 years)	0.23
Children (11–12 years)	0.25
Children (13–15 years)	0.27

Source: Atkinson, A.B. (1970), On the measurement of inequality, *Journal of Economic Theory* 2, pp. 244–263.

TABLE 2.10 Examples of the McClements Scale in Operation

Household Membership	*Raw GMHI*	*McClements Scale*	*Equivalised GMHI*
Single occupant	£1,000	0.61	£1,639
Couple in marital or cohabiting relationship	£1,000	1.00 (0.61 + 0.39)	£1,000
Two friends living together	£1,000	1.07 (0.61 + 0.46)	£935
Couple in a cohabiting relationship, with one of their parents	£1,000	1.42 (0.61 + 0.39 + 0.42)	£704
Couple in a cohabiting relationship, with 9-year-old twins and a 6-year-old child	£1,000	1.67 (0.61 + 0.39 + 0.23 + 0.23 + 0.21)	£599

the fact that the McClements Scale is more than just a headcount – it attempts to model (in a very simple way) the extent to which different household members add to the living costs of the household (e.g. two non-cohabiting friends would be unlikely to share a bedroom compared to two cohabiting adults).

The original real income data is then corrected to reflect household expenditures by dividing it by the McClements Scale score for that household; the resulting income value is termed 'equivalised income'. **Table 2.10** demonstrates the calculations for some hypothetical households (Atkinson, 1970).

Therefore, as a household increases in the number of its members, or in terms of how 'expensive' its members are, its McClements Scale score increases and its equivalised income decreases – two cannot live as cheaply as one; therefore, a larger/more expensive household requires more initial income to have a similar equivalised income (or standard of living) as a smaller/less expensive household.[3] Another way of interpreting the data in **Table 2.10** is that a household containing only one person can live as well on £1,000 per month as a household containing a couple can live on £1,639 pounds per month.

Does the equivalisation of raw income data make a large difference to the household income data within the UKHLS? **Figure 2.2** certainly suggests that it might well do so. On the horizontal axis, **Figure 2.2** measures the various McClements Scale scores that households may correspond to (ranging from 0.61 for a single person household to a maximum of 6.27 for a larger household with many members) while on the vertical axis we measure how many households match that specific McClements Scale score.[4]

Some households match to a McClements Scale score of more than six – for such households, their real gross monthly household monthly income (GMHI) level overstates by a factor of more than six, the standard of living that their income is able to obtain for them; even setting aside these extreme and low-frequency scores, it is still possible to find examples of high-frequency scores that would still imply that household composition has a significant impact on the standard of living that such households could finance from their household incomes. Thus, in Wave A of

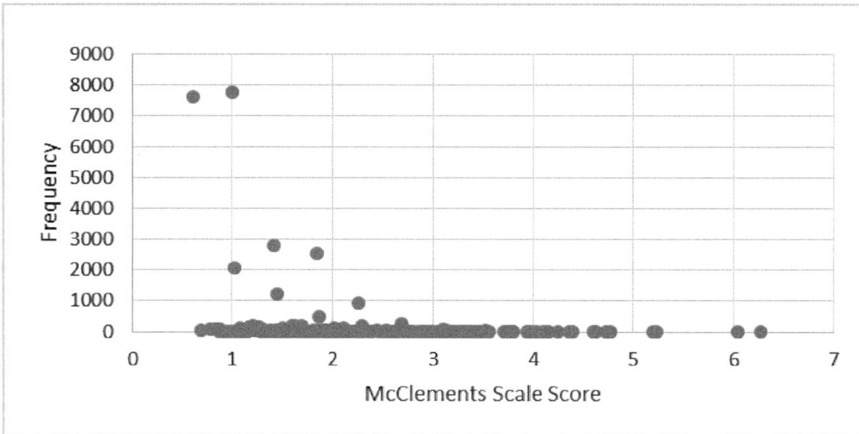

FIGURE 2.2 UKHLS distribution of McClements scale scores

the UKHLS dataset, 2,807 (16.1%) of the households contain a couple in a marital or cohabiting relationship plus a third adult, resulting in a McClements Scale score of 1.42 (derived from combining the individual McClements Scores 0.61 + 0.39 + 0.42). This represents a 42% cut in potential household income that would be felt in comparison with a household with just two cohabiting adults with the same initial (raw) starting household income before equivalisation.

Using equivalised rather than unequivalised real monthly household income levels has important implications for the understanding of the nature of income inequality, poverty and wealth because of the differential effects that equivalising income has on different household types. Equivalisation of household income re-orders households within the income distribution. Larger households with the same initial household income as a smaller household will move lower down the income distribution after equivilisation. As a result, the incidence of poverty will increase in larger households and a focus on poverty is more identified within larger households. This will, in many cases, be households with larger numbers of children, and whose poverty may well remain hidden if only unequivalised income is considered. Focusing on equivalised income may ensure that policy proposals for poverty alleviation are potentially also more effective in tackling the most pressing cases of households without the ability to purchase basic goods needed to live for many of the most vulnerable in a society.

Table 2.11 provides information on equivalised real GMHI across our five waves of data within the UKHLS in comparison with the data for the unequivalised real GMHI presented earlier in **Table 2.7**. As with the real GMHI data, we find that there is a little change over this period with mean equivalised gross monthly household income (eGMHI rising from £2,551 per month to £2,597 per month (a 1.8% increase) from Wave A to Wave E). Thus, as with the previous evidence of real household income changes, this was a period of stagnant income. This consistency between our two measures of mean monthly household income

TABLE 2.11 UKHLS Real Gross Monthly Household Income (Unequivalised and Equivalised) 2010–2014

Wave	*A*	*B*	*C*	*D*	*E*	*Mean A to E*
Mean GMHI	£2,909	£2,934	£2,958	£2,934	£2,939	£2,935
Mean equivalised GMHI	£2,551	£2,574	£2,578	£2,587	£2,597	£2,577
N	30,169	30,508	27,782	25,875	24,369	

Source: UKHLS Waves A–E (2010–2014).

is not surprising since there were only small changes in the household composition and real income data in **Tables 2.3** and **2.7**, respectively. The fact that mean values of equivalised real GMHI are lower than those for unequivalised real GMHI naturally follows from the fact that McClements Scale scores are more likely to lie above one than they are to lie below one. Although the equivalised real GMHI data are stable across this period, the equivalisation process has led to significant re-ordering within the income distribution. Chapters 2 and 3 examine the implications of the re-ordering of households within the income distribution occurring as a result of equivilisation of household income.

Pre- and post-housing cost measures

The next consideration of income date required before it can be used in any analysis is to take into account regional variation of major expenditure, specifically housing costs. For many households, the main element of their household expenditure is their housing costs, whether in the form of mortgage or rent payments. Although households may be thought to have some degree of freedom on how much they choose to spend on housing, the composition and availability of housing in an area of residence can place strong constraints on that freedom, particularly within the short term. The literature on poverty and inequality identifies household income after housing costs (or 'net' income) as a more generally accepted measure of disposable income since this indicates how much actual income remains to be spent on items other than housing.

Table 2.12 adds an additional row to our **Table 2.11**, presenting data on income for households in the UKHLS net of housing costs. The new income

TABLE 2.12 UKHLS Equivalised Real Gross Monthly Household Income Before and After Housing Costs 2010–2014

Wave	*A*	*B*	*C*	*D*	*E*	*Mean A to E*
Mean unequivalised GMHI	£2,909	£2,934	£2,958	£2,934	£2,939	£2,935
Mean equivalised eGMHI	£2,551	£2,574	£2,578	£2,587	£2,597	£2,577
Mean equivalised eNMHI	£1,966	£2,078	£2,092	£2,100	£2,125	£2.072
N	30,169	30,508	27,782	25,875	24,369	

Source: UKHLS Waves A–E (2010–2014).

variable, equivalised Net Household Monthly Income (eNMHI) has had two corrections applied to it – the removal of the income used to pay housing costs, and the equivalisation for household composition. The household income figure that results from applying these two corrections depends on the order in which they are applied. In the analysis for this study, housing costs are removed first, and then equivalisation is applied, on the basis that households pay their (non-equivalised) mortgage/rent out of your non-equivalised income, not your equivalised income used for consumption.

As per previous household income measures, **Table 2.11** demonstrates that there is a small increase in the eNHMI variable over these years. However, in rising from £1,966 to £2,125 per month from Wave A to Wave E, an 8.1% rise, the increase is somewhat larger than seen in our other measures.

Inequality

With a consistent measure of household income, standardised for inflation, household size, and housing costs, the UKHLS provide a consistent income variable which allows for the study of income inequality across the sampled population. In the chapters that follow we will look at the changing patterns of distribution by household types over time and the impact a redistribution of income has on these households' incidence of poverty and inequality. In order to do so requires a mechanism to quantify these changes. The measure used in this book to quantify the impact of these transfers of income is based upon a concept of the Lorenz curve and its linkage to a measure of inequality, the Gini coefficient.

Lorenz curves and Gini coefficients

The main foci of this book are poverty and inequality in the UK – a situation where some households have more income than others. To examine inequality, we need to be able to measure it and present that information in a meaningful way. While a variety of methods for doing so can be adopted most, in one form or another, seek to capture the linkage between the top and the bottom of the income distribution. One of the most useful representations of these differences is through the use of a Lorenz curve, as shown in **Figure 2.3**.

In the context of household income, a Lorenz curve can be understood as follows. Households are ordered from left to right on the horizontal axis according to their household income with the lowest income households on the left and the highest-income households on the right. Lorenz curves show what percentage of all households' income is received by households up to that point on the horizontal axis. The 'line of equality' (rising at 45° to the horizontal axis) would be the Lorenz curve for a sample of households whose incomes were all equal-perfect equality; the bottom x% of households in terms of income would have x% of all income. However, almost all imaginable samples of households would some degree of inequality, and this would result in a Lorenz curve where the bottom

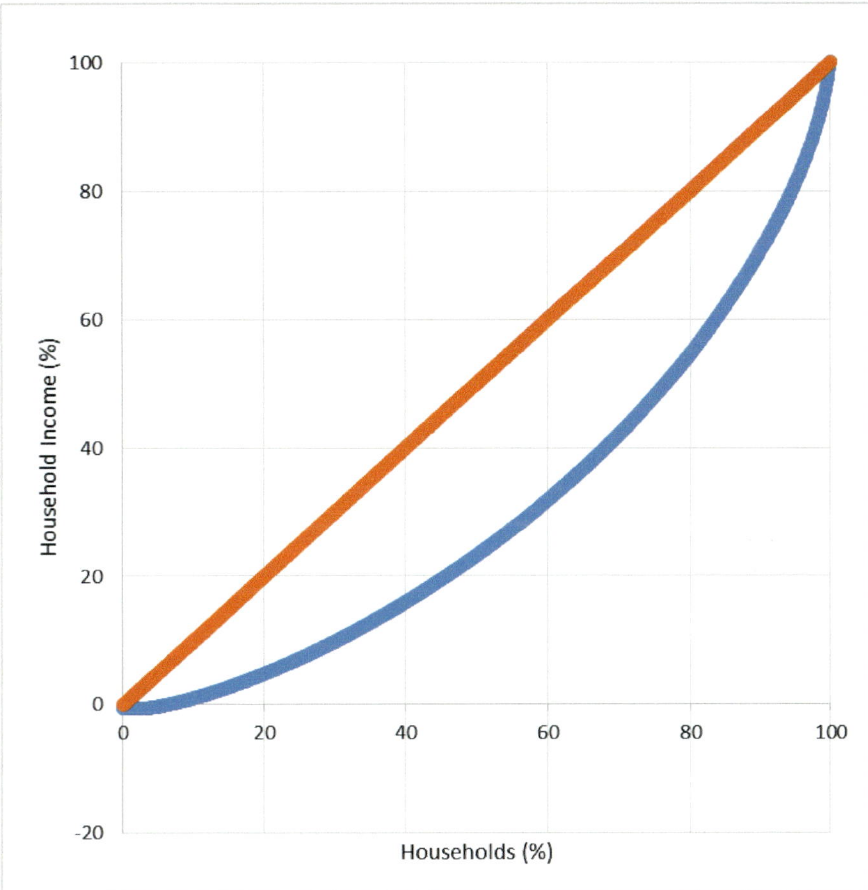

FIGURE 2.3 Lorenz curve of UKHLS equivalised Net Monthly Household Income

x% of households in terms of income would have less than x% of all household income. The more unequal is the sample of households in terms of their income, the further below the 'line of equality' will be the Lorenz curve for that sample of households (i.e. the more 'convex' the Lorenz curve would be to the right).

The Lorenz curve for Wave A of the UKHLS using equivalised eNHMI data is presented in **Figure 2.3**, which clearly shows that there is inequality in the panel dataset. The poorest 20% of households receive only 4.83% of all household income, and even if we extend this to the poorest 40%, their share rises to only 15.93%; the greater income of this second tranche of households reflects the fact that we have ordered households according to their income, and so as we move along the horizontal axis from left to right, we are observing fewer poor households.

Casual observation of the Lorenz curve in **Figure 2.3** might lead one to think that it starts out at zero and then increases from there on as we add more households and their associated income, although income increases only slowly to begin with since these initial households are poor. However, we noted earlier in this chapter that the income of some households was in fact negative (e.g. due to losses from self-employment businesses, etc.), and so in reality the Lorenz curve dips below the horizontal axis for a small number of households before rising above it.

The visual effect of the divergence from equality contained within a Lorenz curve ensures that the concept of inequality can be readily understood. Statisticians have, however, developed a more precise way of quantifying this divergence from equality presented by a Lorenz curve in the estimation of a Gini coefficient. With reference to **Figure 2.3**, the area between the blue and orange lines (A) and the area below the blue line (B), the Gini coefficient for income data can be calculated as:

$$Gini\ Coefficient = \frac{A}{A+B} \tag{2.4}$$

How do changes in income inequality feed through the Lorenz curve into the Gini coefficient? As income inequality increases, the Lorenz curve is initially flattered since the poorest households receive a smaller proportion of all household income, before subsequently becoming steeper later on since the richest households receive a bigger proportion; ultimately, however, it must end up at the same point because 100% of households must be in receipt of 100% of household income. Thus, greater income inequality must be associated with a Lorenz curve further away from the line of equality and therefore the area represented by 'A' must rise and the area represented by 'B' must fall; thus, the Gini coefficient must rise because its numerator (A) rises but its denominator (A + B) does not change. For purely mathematical reasons, the Gini coefficient must lie within the range 0–1 inclusive; a value of 0 would imply perfect equality (the Lorenz curve would be the line of equality, therefore A would be equal to zero and the Gini coefficient would become 0 ÷ B = 0), while a value of 1 would imply perfect inequality (one household had all of the income, B would be zero, and so the Gini coefficient would become A ÷ A = 1).

Therefore, it has become common practice to summarise the inequality evident in a Lorenz curve by presenting the associated Gini coefficient instead, with a value closer to 0 indicating greater equality. However, two caveats should be noted. First, although a specific Lorenz curve always generates a specific Gini coefficient, the reverse does not hold – a specific Gini coefficient can be obtained from different Lorenz curves. A change in a Gini coefficient requires some additional information, such as a change in the median income in order to indicate which part of the income distribution is subject to adjustment. **Table 2.13** presents Gini coefficients for eNHMI for five waves of the UKHLS data and shows an initial decline between Waves A and C associated with a rise in mean NMHI indicating that the rising mean income was concentrated in the lower end of the income distribution before the Gini coefficient rose again in Wave D as mean

TABLE 2.13 UKHLS Gini Coefficients for eNMHI 2010–2014

Wave	*A*	*B*	*C*	*D*	*E*	*Mean A to E*
Mean equivalised NMHI	£1,966	£2,078	£2,092	£2,100	£2,125	£2.072
Gini Coeff eNMHI	0.40367	0.37065	0.35457	0.35844	0.35535	0.36854
N	30,169	30,508	27,782	25,875	24,369	

Source: UKHLS Waves A–E (2010–2014).

monthly household income stagnated. The Gini coefficients for waves D and E, therefore, indicates that the improvement in the lower end of the income distribution in previous years was a temporary phenomenon.[5]

The second caveat concerns the presence of negative numbers in the data (i.e. negative household income in the case of the UKHLS). The Gini coefficient is intended to be calculated on the basis of non-negative data, and the presence of negative data within a sample will result in the Gini coefficient being biased upwards; in extreme cases, the Gini coefficient may even rise above one. On the basis of the Lorenz curve in **Figure 2.3**, the extent of this bias in Gini coefficients calculated from the eNHMI data within the UKHLS is likely to be limited.[6]

Correlation and Causation

The final additional statistical analysis undertaken with the UKHLS dataset within this study is the use of Ordinary Least Square regression analysis (OLS) to test for the existence of correlation and subsequently causation between the variables used within the dataset. Regression analysis is a means of estimating the best fit in the relationship between a set of variables. The regressions presented in the chapters within this book (see example 2.5) use the basic form of the Gini coefficient as the dependent variable and the data on household income, household characteristics and to test for statistical dependencies.

$$GINI = \alpha(eNMHI) + \beta\,(Household) + cons \tag{2.5}$$

Where *GINI* is our dependent variable, the Gini coefficient *eNMHI* is our measure of equivalised net monthly household income net of housing costs, *Household* is our measure of household characteristics and *cons* is our error term. The correlation coefficients are then α and β respectively. Within different chapters, this basic form is then augmented with additional relevant variables.

A positive correlation coefficient on the variables in the regression results suggests that the variable and the Gini coefficient adjust synchronously while a negative correlation coefficient suggests the variable and the Gini coefficient are inversely related. The reliability of this statistical relationship is then provided by the t- or z-statistic result from the regression. For readers unfamiliar with regression analysis, for a variable to be positively correlated with another, their coefficient must have a positive sign and to be statistically significant at the 5% level a t- or z-statistic greater or equal to 1.94 is required. The higher the t- or z-statistic, the more statistically significant a variable is considered to be (Carter Hill, Griffiths and Judge, 1997).

Thus, using OLS linear regressions, the statistical reliability of the relationships between variables within the data can be examined. In the following chapters it is also possible to use a specific form of OLS regression by augmenting the basic form with dummy variables in logit regression analysis, to extend this statistical relationship further to examine the causality of these relationships.

Conclusion

The above chapter sought to introduce the data contained in the UKHLS and some key concepts related to the statistical analysis of the household study data. The UKHLS's inter-temporal consistency provides a unique longitudinal survey of individuals within households. Aggregating these individual sets of data into households provides us with a variable that permits comparable assessment of the changes in these households over the years of the data examined. To do so requires an understanding of a small number of relatively intuitive statistical concepts. This book is not aimed at a highly specialised statistical examination but rather to introduce the opportunities for research to a wider readership. The use of averages combined with Gini coefficients provides sufficient assessment of changes within the whole of the income distribution at the household level to draw valuable and far-reaching conclusions for our understanding of poverty, wealth and inequality within the UK. This can then be extended further to examine the statistical reliability of these correlations through the use of OLS linear regression analysis to demonstrate that these relationships arise from causation not simple correlation. The book now turns to examine a series questions related to poverty, wealth and inequality in the UK. Together these provide examples of the mechanism by which a longitudinal dataset can provide evidence of not only the incidence of poverty and inequality but also its resilience to change.

Notes

1 Thus income truncation at £20,000 per month is applied not only to households with positive GMHI but also to households with negative GMHI; although no such households appear in Wave A of the UKHLS, very small numbers of such households do appear in subsequent waves.
2 A continuous variable is one where there is scope for values to be very similar but not quite identical. Thus, for example, income levels could differ by as little as one penny, and so be viewed by the mode as being different. A discrete variable, on the other hand, has a limited number of values that it can take and so the mode might well be a more meaningful measure in that instance (an example would be the number of children in a household – you can have 1, 2, 3 and so on, but not 1.0001).
3 The fact that the McClements Scale score for a household containing only a couple in a marital or cohabiting relationship has a score of 1 indicates that such households are implicitly viewed as being a 'norm', and all other households compositions are measured

relative to that norm. The advantage that the McClements Scale has over a simple head-count measure is that it also attempts to capture the potential for economies of scale in households whereby household members may share bedrooms, items such as clothing can be handed down and food can be bought more cheaply in bulk.

4 The very large number of possible household compositions ensures that there are a very large number of possible McClements Scale scores. Most individual scores will match to very few households in the UKHLS sample (perhaps even only one household), though some households (e.g. single occupant households) will match to several thousand households; households with only a couple in a marital or cohabiting relationship (with the McClements Scale score of 1) was the most common.

5 Calculating Gini coefficients in practice necessitates the use of routines within statistical packages such as SPSS or STATA and is beyond the scope of this book and therefore throughout the book the results of the analysis are simply reported.

6 To test the consistency of the Gini coefficient to alternative approaches in dealing with negative income data, the authors estimated Gini coefficients to slightly different versions of the data. First, alternative approach was to replace all negative income data with values of zero. This obtained a Gini coefficient of 0.39504. The second alternative approach was to remove from the sample, all households with negative income. This obtained a Gini coefficient of 0.38631. Two conclusions can be drawn. First, it confirms that the presence of negative income data (as in the original version of the UKHLS data) raises the Gini coefficient. Second, although the Gini coefficients for the alternative samples are reduced compared to that for the original sample, the alternative Gini coefficients are not broadly similar.

References

Atkinson, A.B. (1970), On the Measurement of Inequality. *Journal of Economic Theory* 2, pp. 244–263.

Carter Hill, R., Griffiths, W.E. and Judge, G.G. (1997), *Undergraduate Econometrics*, New York: John Wiley & Sons.

De Vos, K. and Asghar Zaidi, M. (1977, September), Equivalence Scale Sensitivity of Poverty Statistics for Member States of the European Community. *Review of Income and Wealth, Series* 43(3), pp. 319–333.

Dorling, D. (2014), *Inequality and the 1%*, London: Verso Publications.

Emmerson, C. and Joyce, R. (2014), *The fiscal squeeze and tax and welfare changes affecting low-earning individuals*, London: Institute of Fiscal Studies.

Jäckle, A., Gaia, A., Al Baghal, T., Burton, J. and Lynn, P. (2017), '*Understanding Society: The UK Household Longitudinal Study Innovation Panel*', *Waves 1–9, User Manual*, Version 1.0, June. University of Essex: Colchester, Essex: Institute for Social and Economic Research.

Lazer, D., Kennedy, R., King, G. and Vespignani, A. (2014, March 14), The Parable of Google Flu: Traps in Big Data Analysis, *Science* 343, pp. 1203–1205.

Martin, R. (2001), Geography and Public Policy: The Case of the Missing Agenda. *Progress in Human Geography* 25(2), pp. 189–120.

Office for National Statistics. (2014), Births in England and Wales, available at https://www.ons.gov.uk/peoplepopulationandcommunity/birthsdeathsandmarriages/livebirths/bulletins/birthsummarytablesenglandandwales/2015-07-15#live-births-numbers-and-rates accessed June 15 2020.

Office for National Statistics. (2015), Retail Price Index, available at https://www.ons.gov.uk/economy/inflationandpriceindices/timeseries/chaw/mm23/previous accessed June 10 2020.

Solesbury, W. (2002), The Ascendency of Evidence, *Planning Theory* 3, pp. 90–96.

3

EXTREME POVERTY

A structural inequality?

Introduction

The initial chapters of this book demonstrated how the UK Household Longitudinal Survey (UKHLS), Understanding Society could uniquely be used to document and chart changing patterns of household poverty, wealth and inequality. The following chapters now address specific case studies in the areas of poverty, wealth and inequality arising from using the data.

This chapter examines the most fundamental characterisation of the poorest within society, namely that their poverty is a result of individual choice or whether it can better understood as a function of the social construction of poverty? In order to examine this question, we use the UKHLS to examine the characteristics of the bottom decile of the income distribution. As Chapter 2 highlighted, the UKHLS allows us to order households by income levels from the poorest to the richest and in doing so examine the bottom decile, the poorest 10% of households. It is in the bottom decile, where we find the very poorest households and where we might expect to find the greatest incidence of the individual characteristics of the long-term poor. Anti-poverty strategies focused upon these groups increasingly have identified the need for behavioural change in order to eradicate poverty. In doing so policies which focus upon individual characteristics may ignore wider social determinants of poverty. In the chapter, we first examine debates over dependency culture and then examine the extent to which these characterisations can be linked to the poorest households through the use of the UKHLS data.

The chapter demonstrates that extremely poor households predominantly fall into specific categories that can be linked to structural, or lifecycle, explanations of poverty rather than with individual choice or failure. The chapter further utilises the composition of the very poorest households in the income distribution

DOI: 10.4324/9781315179957-3

in order to highlight that many of the common characterisations of poverty as dependency are also misplaced. The UKHLS data not only points towards structural explanations for poverty but further that these household characteristics are also predictors of the immobility of the poorest households in escaping extreme poverty. One particular group identified in the data identified in this chapter are those households that contain an adult carer. Those with caring responsibilities are both disproportionately represented within the bottom 10% of households, by income, but are also among the least mobile with respect to changing their income levels over time. The conclusion emerging from this approach is that the conceptualisation of poverty as a discourse of choice and dependency creates a barrier to a genuine understanding of the reality of poverty and acts as an impediment to examining potential remedies that offer a genuine opportunity to achieve a real change in the income distribution.

A deserving and undeserving poor

Patterns of inequality and poverty and their damaging effects on individuals have been well documented by official government bodies and social scientists within the UK. Government survey work produces data that forms the basis for social research into income-related poverty. The *Family Resource Survey* and the *Households Below Average Income* household panel survey are among the most widely recognised and useful sources of individual and household-level data. It is these sources that provide the basis for much of the quantitative research into poverty and inequality with, for example, the Joseph Rowntree Foundation (JRF) utilising these sources in publishing its annual *Monitoring Poverty and Social Exclusion* series. A general characterisation of income-related poverty and inequality suggests a marked worsening since the 1970s with the improvement during the early 1990s before falling back, despite growth within the economy. As the JRF noted in 2008 of the 30 indicators of poverty and inequality which saw improvement in the first five years of the 1990s, 15 of them saw no further improvement, with the low-income statistics specifically being characterised by 'stagnation then deterioration' (Palmer, MacInnes and Kenway, 2008, p. 12). Since 2008 in the aftermath of the Great Financial Crash and the advent of austerity, the 2011 report noted the continued failures to address income poverty and inequality with any improvement only identifiable in poverty among pensioners and households with children (Aldridge, Parekh, MacInnes and Kenway, 2011, Table 2). The 2016 edition noted that the figure of 21% of the population living in low-income households had barely changed since 2002, while other indicators for income poverty had again worsened (Tinson, Ayrton, Barker, Barry Born, Aldridge and Kenway, 2016, Figure 4).

The desire to distinguish between the stock and the flow of poverty within society has been a goal of social policy throughout its history. Dating back as far as the Elizabethan Poor Law, in-door relief within the confines of a workhouse was designed to identify and 'correct' the moral failings of the poor and separate them from those in genuine need who would be granted out-door relief. Jeremy Bentham in the nineteenth century provided the terminology of a distinction between the 'deserving' and 'undeserving' poor, which was embodied in the twentieth century with the rise of insurance-based systems of social security. More generous insurance-based social security for the temporary poor provided payments over and above the welfare provided for the long-term poor, who would instead be solely reliant upon more meagre state-provided welfare. The insurance-based approach was a principal of Beveridge's reforms establishing the post-war welfare state (Fraser, 1989). From the end of the twentieth century, the concept of 'conditionality', the need to demonstrate compliance in behaviour or risk draconian sanctions to withdraw welfare, provided a modern terminology and form for Benthamite ideology. The central conceptualisation of poverty within the liberal framework is therefore of individual failure or deviance from expected norms of behaviour. Corrective change, voluntary or otherwise, is therefore required to bring about change in circumstances for those facing poverty. Government policy, therefore, while delivering immediate support, is embedded within a requirement to prevent recipients of support from maintaining anything resembling an adequate standard of living and maintains their position on the margins of society. As we see in Chapter 4 on wealth, such conceptualisation and requirement for behavioural change are not applied to the richest in society.

That a level of extreme poverty exists is thus not disputed among social science and policy researchers; however, this long-observed existence of a section of the population classed as poor, which appears intransigent to social policy, has given rise to a wide range of interpretations for its persistence which continues to focus upon the dichotomy between deserving and undeserving (Dorling, 2010). Indeed, the explanation for such a minority facing abject poverty, alongside a variety of failed remedies for this poverty, is however subject to much politicised and conflicting debate.

One explanation for this existence of extreme poverty lies with a permanent fracturing of the role played by work in society. The urban riots in England during 2011 saw the linking of this section of the poor with that of a more deep-rooted decay in society, with the description of a 'slow-motion moral collapse that has taken place in parts of our country these past few generations' by the then Prime Minister David Cameron MP (Lewis, Taylor and Ball, 2011). David Starkey, the populist academic went further, invoking racist ideology to suggest that this 'feral' underclass of young white working-class rioters had degenerated into becoming 'black' (*sic*) (Guardian, 2011a). While such extreme descriptions are contested (witness complaints from academics over Starkey's outburst (Guardian, 2011b; Jones, 2011), the view of an underclass separated off from a wider society is a view that has more academically serious and often progressive support. A precariously employed new class formation, a 'precariat', is generated by its dislocation from traditional work patterns (full-time, permanent employment), and marks it out from other sub-sections of the working class.

This precariat is also socially fixed in its position through a lack of opportunity and mobility. Standing (2011) maintains that the precariat's lack of access to higher skilled and higher-paid work that would give rise to individual advancement, or through a lack of access to higher pay in their existing employment via trade union collective action, precludes access to a more secure or prosperous future. Thus, the precariat becomes a class fraction separated off from a wider working class. Such depictions of insecurity are challenged by Doogan (2009) who suggests that many of the changes identified reflect the greater participation in paid work by sections of the population, particularly women, who were previously outside the labour force, and is therefore, a sign of greater rather than lesser employment stability. The work of Aldridge et al. (2011, p. 78), *Monitoring Poverty and Social Exclusion,* identified under-employment affecting six million people by 2011, over 10% of the UK workforce, as its highest level since 1993. Office for National Statistics (2019) figures for underemployment demonstrate that at 7.6% in 2019, the figure is almost identical to the official unemployment rate of 7.5%. This noticeable emergence of part-time working and self-employment alongside unemployment, particularly in response to the economic crisis since 2007, suggests that at the bottom end of the income distribution is a section of the population whose response to labour market shocks is not distinct from the rest of the population. Indeed, underemployment in large part is to a hidden degree of unemployment (Choonara, 2019, pp. 63–79).

An alternative to explanations of poverty deriving from the precariousness of work is one that focuses upon worklessness (Dilnot, Kay and Morris, 1984). Government social policy has made repeated attempts to 'target' those households in which a welfare 'dependency culture' is suggested to have emerged. While in 1980 high marginal tax rates, at the income boundary between welfare and work, were identified for the creation of poverty traps affecting 600,000 households, a re-focus upon individual responsibility shifted the focus to dependency (Barr and Coulter, 1990, pp. 328–329). A 'dependency culture' has been suggested to result in a cross-generational transference of worklessness and 'welfare dependency' in the view of Barnet (1986). An emphasis upon incentivising the long-term poor into mainstream economic activity through work as a route out of poverty has therefore been the centrepiece of policy proposals for over three decades beginning with changes to access to unemployment benefits in the 1980s for those deemed to be voluntarily unemployed. The 'seeking work' criteria then became more stringent with the 'actively seeking work' test introduced into the 1995 Jobseekers Act. The Act defined actively seeking work to be:

> such steps as he [*sic*] can reasonably be expected to have to take in order to have the best prospects of securing employment.
>
> *(UK Government, 1995, section 7)*

Since 2012 following the introduction of Universal Credit and extensive use of sanctioning, by the removal of benefits for those deemed to be non-compliant, the 'actively seeking work' test became even more stringent with monitoring and evidence requirements placed upon the unemployed. Together these tests have stigmatised worklessness and drawn the connection between individual failure and poverty. Fletcher and Wright (2018) maintain the neo-liberal coercive nature of universal credit is designed to not only 'criminalise the poor' but to extend this criminalisation beyond a recalcitrant undeserving minority into the wider population (2018, p. 339). Thus, the concept of a deserving and undeserving poor relocates the interpretation of 'deserving' into the employed workforce in the form of underemployment and now provides the new defining feature for policies distinguishing between the two groups with the undeserving, those without work, facing increasing punishment and criminalisation (Wacquant, 2009).

Unsurprisingly, moves to exempt the poor from draconian monitoring and conditionality has arisen by demands to provide a recognition that many unpaid social activities, from volunteering to carer roles. The need to extend the recognition of 'work' beyond labour that generates payment has led to proposals for a Universal Basic Income (UBI). UBI is understood to be a non-means tested minimum income to all citizens deemed to be sufficient to provide a basic level of social security, irrespective of participation in paid work. Within the UK, the Scottish Government has begun consideration of the introduction of a pilot approach to evaluate the effectiveness of such a policy (Goodman and Danson, 2019).

Poor households as lacking incentives?

The consensus of social policy thinking within government emerging from this picture of historically and persistently high levels of income poverty and inequality was the identification of a route out of poverty primarily through paid employment (Dilnot, 1995, p. 10). Here repeated governments, irrespective of political persuasion, pursued an approach that sought to incentivise those in poverty to undertake paid employment through increasing the attractiveness of even low paid work. The introduction of a Minimum Wage in 1998 and Working Families Tax Credits in 2003 (CPAG, 2003, p. 436 and p. 1239) were two examples of this approach. The publication of the 2006 Government Green Paper, *A New Deal for Welfare: Empowering People to Work* was perhaps the clearest enunciation of this view. As the then Secretary of State for Work and Pensions John Hutton MP wrote:

> Compared to 1997, an extra 2.4 million more people are in work and the employment rate for people of working age now stands at almost 75 percent – something which would have been considered unachievable throughout the 1980s and early 1990s. We have managed to make a real difference to millions of lives and to many communities.
>
> *(DWP, 2006, p. 6)*

The conflation of employment with escaping poverty was overplayed in the analysis with the result that a new high level of in-work poverty developed replacing worklessness as the primary characteristic of low-income households. Thus, the 2016 *Monitoring Poverty and Social Exclusion* noted that a record proportion, at 55%, of people living in poverty, were now in households that included working adults (Tinson et al., 2016, Figure 4). Indeed, the responsiveness of the poor to these policies might be recognised by the fact that the United Kingdom's historically high-labour force participation rates did not fall in the 2008 recession following the great Financial Crash as most commentators expected (Bertram and Wright, 2012).

Despite the growing evidence of in-work poverty, the dominance of the 'work as a route out of poverty' ideology has ensured that this approach has become embedded further into welfare policy by the introduction of a 'Work Capability Assessment' for disabled adults as a requirement of receipt of Employment and Support Allowance in 2008. The Work Capability Assessment has been designed to ensure that a new group of long-term welfare claimants, this time the disabled, are now encouraged, or forced, into the labour market (Department for Work and Pensions, 2018).

A further noted consequence of the increasing levels of coercion in welfare policy has been the emergence of rising self-employment rates have since 2007, with 4.1 million workers registering as self-employed by 2013, 16% of all economically active adults (Office of National Statistics [ONS], 2015). Underemployment within this group is particularly prevalent, indicating that high levels of underemployment act to mask the true picture of the fully unemployed (ONS, 2019).

Yet, despite the large impact these changes have had on labour market participation rates income-related poverty and inequality have not abated and remain at historically high levels. It is to critically examine this approach of incentives-based welfare that this chapter now focuses by examining the extent to which those with most to gain from these incentives, those at the very bottom of the income distribution, have household characteristics that are likely to allow them to engage with the work as a route out of poverty approach. The employment route approach implies that employment is open to all household types and therefore those households lowest down the income distribution have the greatest potential gain from an increase in labour market participation.

If, on the other hand, these households are at the bottom of the income distribution for other reasons, such as features of the labour market or factors that are linked to the structures of households themselves, then increasing the incentives into work will offer little assistance in achieving a work-related route out of their poverty. Under these circumstances, introducing greater penalties for those remaining within the welfare system exacerbates poverty with disadvantaged households unable to change their behaviour yet facing increasing coercion for non-compliance.

The discussion below is focused upon income-related improvements but readers should be aware that other improvements such as health, education and wider social inclusion deriving from increasing equality could also prove to be important outcomes of addressing extreme household poverty (Townsend and Davidson, 1992; Wilkinson and Pickett, 2009).

Who are the very poorest in society?

As described in Chapter 2, this study utilises the annual waves of the UKHLS to undertake an examination of equalised real household monthly income net of housing costs. The dataset is first grouped by household composition and then by equivalisation of real gross household income (after housing costs) using the McClements scale provides comparable income data. These undertakings then permit the ordering of the data from lowest income to highest income and thus into income deciles.[1] In this chapter, we use the first five waves of the UKHLS (Wave A to Wave E) covering the period 2010–2014 to focus upon the bottom income decile, i.e. the lowest 10% of households ranked by incomes, and its relationship to those above it. Extreme poverty is thus equated with a household being present in the bottom decile of the household income distribution.

The analysis starts by identifying different household characteristics, or typologies, that may suffer from extreme poverty. By matching household typologies with individual-level data in our sample, we seek to provide explanations for the presence of households within the bottom decile of the household income distribution. In so doing our analysis seeks to examine the relevance of incentives for these households. We then use Wave B data to identify the strength of the statistical relationship between household typologies of being in the bottom decile compared with the same typology's likelihood of being in higher income deciles. Wave B is chosen as the starting point for this analysis as the chapter then moves on to an examination of not only a household's current bottom decile status but also their potential entry into, and their potential exit, from it. In order to do this, we need to make use of the unique longitudinal panel nature of the UKHLS. Our analysis uses Wave B as our 'base year', and therefore the source of our data when using regression analysis to examine the household's current bottom decile status. When we subsequently examine a household's potential entry into the bottom decile, we will examine changes between Waves A and B, and then when we examine their potential exit from the bottom decile, we will exam changes between Waves B and those of Waves C, D and E.

We can characterise households within the bottom decile by household typology. In **Table 3.1**, households are aggregated into nine non-exclusive typologies – (i) pensioners, (ii) carers, (iii) households with low wage rates or hours of work (i.e. 'inadequate employment'), (iv) disability benefit recipients, (v) adult students, (vi) self-employed, (vii) lone parents, (viii) households reliant upon savings "wealth-rich, income-poor" and (ix) unemployed. These nine typologies are themselves aggregated from a longer list of 33 different characteristics (see Appendix 3, **Table A3.1**).

TABLE 3.1 UKHLS Average Percentage of Households in the Bottom Income Decile by Household Typology 2010–2014

Equivalised Household Typologies★	*Decile One*
Pensioner(s)★★	21.5%
Carer(s)	21.1%
Low wage rates and/or limited hours	22.7%
Disability benefit recipient(s)	9.2%
Student(s)★★★	16.8%
Self-employed	16.4%
Lone parents	1.0%
Wealth rich, income poor★★★★	5.9%
Unemployed people	21.1%
None of the above	8.6%
Total★	144.3%

Source: UK Household Longitudinal Survey, Waves A to E covering the period 2010–2014.

★ This table does not treat household typologies as being mutually exclusive, and so the columns of percentages will aggregate to more than 100%. Thus, a household with pensioner, who is a carer for another individual is classified as *both* a pensioner *and* a carer.

★★ Retired people not in receipt of a pension are classified as pensioners in the UKHLS.

★★★ Students are defined as aged 16 or above.

★★★★ Wealth rich, income poor is chosen, by the authors, to be households in which investment income is greater than 17% of all household income and therefore have significant wealth.

While most of the household typologies within a broad category are mutually exclusive (e.g. a household cannot simultaneously be both a single adult carer household and a multiple adult carer household), households can be present in more than one broad typology (e.g. it can contain an individual, or individuals, who are both a pensioner and a carer). Therefore, adding together the incidence of household typologies in each year exceeds 100%. In the case of the UKHLS, the final column of **Table A3.1**, and summarised in **Table 3.1**, shows an average of 144.3%, across five waves of UKHLS data, aggregated households are identified. Thus, almost half of all households have more than one typology.

Table 3.1, demonstrates the variation of household typology located within the bottom decile over five waves of the UKHLS dataset. The nine typologies (households containing pensioners, carers, employees with low wages or part-time employment, disability benefit(s) recipients, students, the self-employed, lone parents, the wealth rich but income poor, and the unemployed) account for 91.4% (100%–8.6%) of all the households' typologies identifiable in the bottom decile across the five years of data. **Table 3.1** shows an analysis that is consistent with an a *priori* belief that specific individuals may be found in extreme poverty. Indeed, of the nine broad categories cover a sizeable number of bottom decile households; inadequate employment (22.7%), pensioners (21.5%), carers (21.1%), unemployment (21.1%), students (16.8%) and self-employed (16.4%), each account for a high proportion of households in the bottom decile. Only a small residual proportion (8.6%) of households in the bottom decile do not fit within one or more of these typologies.

In a society with less than perfect income equality, it is inevitable that some households will be found in the bottom decile, and any policy prescriptions that simply re-orders households within the income distribution will still result in a bottom decile. However, it is necessary to compare the relative presence of these different household typologies in the bottom decile in order to make judgements on the success or otherwise of government welfare policies. While **Table 3.1** evidences household typologies, it is not sufficient evidence that there is a statistical relationship between these household typologies and a household being present in the bottom decile.

It is therefore a requirement to examine the extent to which these household typologies are unequally distributed. In order to examine the extent to which causation can be identified, we can examine the likelihood of specific household typologies appearing in the bottom income decile compared to other income deciles. A logit regression model allows for the analysis of a statistical relationship between a household's bottom decile status and the various possible household typologies. Using Wave B data, a dependent dummy variable (0,1) was used whereby 0 represents households in the bottom decile for equivalised net monthly household income and 1 represents households in the other nine deciles.[2] The results identify the probability of a household type being in the bottom decile. The dependent variables are as previously shown, the 33 household scenarios, plus six control variables.[3] Given the nature of the dependent variable, any household scenario that is statistically more significantly likely to be characteristic of a bottom decile household would elicit a negative coefficient and significant z-statistic in these logit results. The full results can again be found in **Table A3.2** while below they are summarised in **Table 3.2** in an aggregated form. A number of strong results emerge that are very much consistent with the *a priori* beliefs that led us to choose this particular set of household scenarios.

Table 3.2 demonstrates that specific household typologies are indeed located in the bottom decile. The unemployed are both more likely to be in the bottom decile (a negative coefficient of −1.455) and this result is statistically significant (a z-statistic of −25.45). Similarly, carers, students, self-employed and those with accumulated wealth but low income are all more prevalent in the bottom decile with a negative coefficient and that these are statistically significant with a z-score greater than +/− 1.96. All four unemployment-related household typologies in **Table A3.2**, as would be expected, significantly increase the likelihood of a household being in the bottom decile. This includes being in a single or multiple adult households and or reporting receipt of unemployment benefits. Such evidence speaks to the inadequate levels of support for those facing unemployment. Similarly, for students, while this might appear to be a particularly transient phase of their life course, nevertheless that students are statistically significantly likely to be over-represented in the lowest income decile – a result that

TABLE 3.2 UKHLS Logistic Regression for being in the Bottom Decile in Wave B (Nine Household Typologies)

Logistic regression	Number of obs = 27,157
	LR chi²(15) = 1271.46
	Prob > chi² = 0.0000
Log likelihood = −8166.8115	Pseudo R^2 = 0.0722

	UK Household Longitudinal Survey UKHLS Wave B (2010)		
*Household Typologies**	*Coefficient*	*Standard Error*	*Z-Statistic*
Pensioner(s)	−0.0723406	.0539184	−1.34
Carer(s)	−1.042357	.0555897	−18.75
Low wage rates and/or limited hours	0.2445884	.0591581	4.13
Disability benefit recipient(s)	0.504368	.0695101	7.26
Student(s)	−0.5963648	.0594915	−10.02
Self-employed	−0.4906131	.0581486	−8.44
Lone parents	0.177681	.2087667	0.85
Wealth rich, income poor	−0.5894289	.0922549	−6.39
Unemployed people	−1.454904	.0571669	−25.45
Constant	99.39531	20.43063	4.87

Source: UK Household Longitudinal Survey, Wave B for 2010.

* For notes, see Table 3.1.

is indicative of the inadequacy of maintenance support and access to benefits for their welfare.

Carers (whether in single or multiple adult households) are significantly more likely to appear in the bottom decile. This is consistent with the view that their caring responsibilities will limit their employment opportunities. Indeed, the fact that the effect is three times stronger in households with only one adult (where the coefficient for single cares is −.2.053 compared to −0.656 in **Table A3.2**) reinforces this view. Levels of carer's allowance and other benefits leave carers in the most poverty inducing income levels. Where there is a multiple adult household, the carer is likely to be an adult caring for a spouse, partner or disabled individual. The preponderance of carers in the bottom decile is particularly significant for three reasons. First, standard equivalising scales provide a means to compare differing sized households but do not take account of the differing costs of living for households of the same size, and therefore do not reflect the additional financial costs associated with caring responsibilities (Thompson, Winfield, Simmons and Linney, 2003). The consequence of this is that the results in **Table 3.2** are likely to be biased downwards and the extent of poverty is still greater than indicated in the data. Second, the additional financial strain of being in the bottom decile is unlikely to be the only stressor on the carer with the additional potential burden of ill-health arising. Finally, it is often the case that the carer's circumstances will remain unchanged in a way that will significantly improve their ability to generate private income or respond to labour market incentives. Indeed, providing long-term care is likely to reduce, rather than enhance, the carer's human capital and, therefore, to a large extent they are increasingly likely to become dependent on the state to support them in their caring activities.

The final two over-represented household typologies are that of the self-employed and those with high levels of income from asset wealth rather than income. In the case of self-employment, the result is driven by the preponderance of single household self-employment (coefficient −0.639 and z-statistic −5.19, **Table A3.2**). Households with multiple self-employed adults are not more likely to be in the bottom decile compared to other income deciles. Such a result is consistent with the view that the growth of self-employment coincides with the increasing coercive approach to those in receipt of unemployment benefits and acts to mask the genuine level of unemployment. In the case of the typology 'wealth rich, income poor,' there are two potential explanations for the result, first that as the typologies are non-exclusive the data identifies pensioners households with accumulated savings and pensions for their income and second self-employed individuals may be using the lower tax rates on dividend payments compared earned income to avoid paying income tax (see Chapter 4 on inequality for more detail).[4]

Table 3.2 also demonstrates that two of the largest household typologies identified in **Table 3.1** are not more likely to the found within the bottom decile than other households. Thus, while households with low wage rates or with limited hours of employment and pensioners contribute 22.7% and 21.5% of households in the bottom decile respectively, they are not found to be disproportionately found to be represented in the bottom decile than elsewhere in the income distribution.

In the case of those with low wage levels and limited hours or work, the coefficient on their prevalence in **Table 3.2** is positive (0.2446), indicating a greater likelihood of being in the higher income deciles relative to bottom income decile and with a z-statistic (4.13) showing this result is statistically significant. However, **Table A3.2** shows that within households with low wage rates or limited hours of work there are specific sub-typologies that, converse to the general result, correlating significantly with being overly represented in the bottom decile. Those reporting being paid less than the minimum wage (coefficient −0.620 and z-statistic −5.11, **Table A3.2**) and with working 16–31 hours of work per week (coefficient −0.0002 and z-statistic −4.96, **Table A3.2**) being two examples. This is consistent with the work of Wills (2009) and others (Standing, 2011; UNISON 2013) who have examined the role of low paid and insecure work in labour market's where segmentation and discrimination exist. The biggest single element of the low-paid typology (10.1% of household typologies see **Table A3.1**) are those adults aged 22–64 who earn less than the statutory Minimum Wage, while a further 5.5% of the bottom decile earn at least the Minimum Wage for their age band, but less than the living wage. Thus, the UKHLS data suggests that the existence of extreme levels of in-work poverty can be identified with higher numbers of hours at work, in low paid employment. Whereas for those working under 16 hours per week, and potentially in receipt of in-work benefits, these households are less likely to be found in the bottom decile (coefficient 0.662 and z-statistic 19.84, **Table A3.2**).

For pensioners, while they have a negative coefficient (−0.072), this is not a statistically significant result (z-statistic 1.34, **Table 3.2**). However, as with the evidence from low paid work, a similar pattern of differentiation in the population is identifiable. While pensioner households overall are found to be more prevalent in the bottom decile, with a negative coefficient, the statistical significance of their aggregated typology, their z-statistic (−1.34), is below the significance level required for confidence in the result. However, while pensioners, in general, are not significantly more represented in the bottom decile, those single or couple pernsioner households whose only recourse is the state pension are highly significantly more likely to be in the bottom decile (for pensioner couple households, coefficient −0.7304 and z-statistic −4.65 are given in **Table A3.2**). Such results indicate that the universal state pension alone is insufficient to provide an income level that removes them from extreme poverty. Conversely, for those pensioner households accessing both the state pension and pension credits (for a single pensioner household, coefficient of 0.787 and a highly significant z-statistic of 3.86 are given in **Table A3.2**) are less likely to be found within those at the very bottom of the income distribution and thus indicates the issue of the entitlement and access to benefits for more vulnerable groups within the pensioner population should be a policy concern.

The evidence derived from UKHLS suggests that the great majority of extreme poverty in households in the UK originates from distinct household typologies. Households in the bottom decile are not evenly distributed, nor similar to poor households with access to greater welfare provision, e.g., disabled and single parents, in higher income deciles. Rather the bottom decile is heavily over-represented by households with distinct characteristics relative to the population as a whole. Households containing adults who are unemployed, carers, students or single adult self-employed constitute the largest groups, collectively accounting for 63% of the 144% (**Table A3.1**) of all household typologies found in the bottom decile. While those with accumulated wealth but low income are also over-represented their absolute numerical proportion, (5.9% in **Table 3.1**) indicates they remain a more marginal household typology.

While this tells us about the statistical significance of those found within the bottom decile, it is not yet sufficient evidence to draw a conclusion that these forms of extreme poverty are structured into society. We need to ascertain if the statistical correlation identified arises from a temporary phenomenon, from the transitory impacts of changes to households, or is a long-lasting effect for those households in extreme poverty? In order to examine this, it is again possible to use the longitudinal aspect of the UKHLS to examine changes in household typologies over time and therefore entry and exit from the bottom decile.

Mobility

While we can identify in the UKHLS, the characteristics of households facing extreme poverty it is also necessary to distinguish between long- and short-term effects. Therefore, it is important to examine the evidence of duration of extreme poverty, as indicated by a household's presence in the bottom decile overtime. It is this feature of the UKHLS that is unique and allows us to move from an understanding of correlation in a single year towards a concept of causation, the social construction of structural poverty via the use of statistical significance.

Table 3.3 shows the results for a similar logic regression analysis previously undertaken above except that on this occasion it uses Waves A and B at the aggregated level of the nine typologies.[5] In this case, the analysis identifies the statistical significance of households moving into the bottom decile at Wave B from outside the bottom decile in Wave A. [6] The logit regression results in **Table 3.3** uses a dependent dummy variable (0,1) where 0 represents households entering into the bottom decile and 1 represents households not doing so. Consistent with previous results a negative coefficient and significant z-statistic indicates a household typology that is statistically more likely to enter the bottom decile. Again, a number of statistically significant results emerge that not only reinforces our knowledge that some household typologies are more commonly found within the bottom income decile, but that the 'acquisition' of these household typologies is associated with the move into the bottom decile.

TABLE 3.3 UKHLS Logistic Regression for Entering into the Bottom Decile in Wave B (Nine Household Typologies)

Logistic regression	Number of obs =17,672		
	LR chi^2(15) = 310.36		
	Prob > chi^2 = 0.0000		
Log likelihood = −4388.8554	Pseudo R^2 = 0.0342		
	UK Household Longitudinal Survey UKHLS Waves A and B (2010 and 2011)		
*Household Typologies**	*Coefficient*	*Standard Error*	*Z-Statistic*
Pensioner(s)	.0816917	.1869712	0.44
Carer(s)	−.3272745	.1181757	−2.77
Low wage rates and/or limited hours	.001234	.0750096	0.02
Disability benefit recipient(s)	.7275612	.1524576	4.77
Student(s)	−.4076431	.1091124	−3.74
Self-employed	−2347544	.1177119	−1.99
Lone parents	1.19058	.1855994	6.41
Wealth rich, income poor	−.5586829	.1351999	−4.13
Unemployed people	−1.128917	.0926172	−12.19
Constant	28.92318	28.14272	1.03

Source: UK Household Longitudinal Survey, Wave A and B (2010–2011).

* For notes, see Table 3.1.

Thus, causation rather than simple correlation can begin to be established for the means by which structural poverty is created.[7]

Table 3.3 consistent with our earlier results indicates that households acquiring one of the five broad typologies previously identified is statistically significantly more likely to enter into the bottom decile by the following wave. Having a negative coefficient and a highly negative z-statistic applies to households containing the unemployed, carers, students, the self-employed and those who are wealth-rich but income-poor. Conversely, the acquisition of Disability Benefits or Lone Parent status, with a positive coefficient and a highly positive z-statistic, statistically reduces the likelihood of entry into the bottom decile. The pensioner and low wages or limited working hours broad typologies have (with low z-statistics) no statistically significant effect.

The results not only indicate that acquiring specific household typologies creates extreme poverty but that other typologies are unlikely to result in extreme poverty. Therefore, access to forms of welfare identifying specific households is sufficient to prevent extreme poverty and therefore the descent into the bottom income decile is indicative of specific forms, or absence of, welfare policy. While entering into the bottom income decile may therefore have structural causes, it still remains to be identified whether these household typologies lead to prolonged levels of structurally induced extreme poverty. Here, it is necessary to examine the exit from the bottom decile.

The next stage therefore in this analysis is the examination of households who exit from the bottom decile. We construct a sample of those households who were in the bottom decile in Wave B and look forward to Waves C, D and E to see whether (and how quickly) they exited from the bottom decile. An ordered logit regression results are provided in **Table 3.4**, where the dependent variable is given a value of either (0,1,2,3), where 3 represents a bottom decile household in Wave B exiting from the bottom decile by Wave C, 2 represents a bottom decile household in Wave B exiting the bottom decile by Wave D and 1 represents a bottom decile household exiting the bottom decile by Wave E. Finally, a value of 0 for the dependent variable represents a bottom decile household who had still not exited the bottom decile by Wave E. This ordering within the dependent variable ensures that those broad typologies of households *least* affected by extreme poverty in the bottom income decile are once more going to be indicated by a positive and significant coefficient – they are more able to exit the bottom decile, and to do so quickly.

Table 3.4 provides the results for this analysis.[8] The results again suggest that there are differential impacts of mobility depending upon the typology of households in the bottom decile. Three groups with a positive coefficient and a high z-statistic possess a statistically significantly better chance of exiting the bottom decile within the time frame than other typologies. First, households possessing low wage rates or limited hours of employment (coefficient 0.473 and z-statistic 2.96) have significantly greater ability to leave the bottom decile; such households may be in the bottom decile as of Wave B because temporarily they could not find employment with higher earnings or more hours, but in due course either their current employment

TABLE 3.4 Ordered Logistic Regression for UKHLS Households Exiting from the Bottom Decile as of Waves C, D or E (Nine Household Typologies)

Ordered logistic regression	Number of obs = 1426		
	LR $chi^2(15) = 56.15$		
	Prob > $chi^2 = 0.0000$		
Log likelihood = −1565.8778	Pseudo $R^2 = 0.0176$		
	UK Household Longitudinal Survey UKHLS Waves B and E (2011–2014)		
Household Typologies★	*Coefficient*	*Standard Error*	*Z-Statistic*
Pensioner(s)	.043658	.13708	0.32
Carer(s)	−.158245	.1372346	−1.15
Low wage rates and/or limited hours	.4728812	.1600139	2.96
Disability benefit recipient(s)	.516553	.1840981	2.81
Student(s)	.2065579	.1567126	1.32
Self-employed	.0863674	.1424782	0.61
Lone parents	−.2547776	.6468768	−0.39
Wealth rich, income poor	−.4970921	.1943039	−2.56
Unemployed people	.4495318	.1477918	3.04
Leave by Wave C	−119.6763	52.01083	
Leave by Wave D	−119.1215	52.00991	
Leave by Wave E	−118.4051	52.00877	

Source: UK Household Longitudinal Survey, Waves B, C, D and E (2011–2014).

★ For notes, see Table 3.1.

improves or they move to better employment. Second, households in receipt of disability benefits have significantly greater ability to leave the bottom decile (coefficient 0.516 and z-statistic 2.81), again indicative of the greater welfare support for those disabled individuals who are deemed to be incapable of work under the Work Capability Assessment test. Third, households suffering from unemployment have significantly better ability to leave the bottom decile (coefficient 0.4495 and z-statistic 3.04) in eventually being able to find employment that offers more in earnings (and in-work benefits) than they could obtain from unemployment-related benefits.

All other broad category households pensioners, carers, students, self-employed and lone parents (other than wealth-rich income-poor ones) generate an insignificant z-statistic (below 1.96) and thus collectively represent the base of immobile household types. Although older people can delay their retirement, once they do enter retirement there is little prospect of bottom decile pensioner households increasing their income sufficiently to exit the bottom decile since their exit from the labour force is likely to be permanent. Similarly, for carers, it is also unlikely that their income will improve unless they cease to be a carer, which is unlikely to happen unless the person they care for moves into an institutional environment or dies. The immobility of student households may stem from the short duration (three years), of the post-entry into decile 1 data used in this aspect of the analysis while the immobility experienced by households with self-employment again is indicative of the rise of self-employment being linked to the increasing conditionality of unemployment benefits. Single-parent households' lack of mobility out of the bottom decile again may reflect the semi-permanence of their household circumstances with children remaining within the household. The only broad category household to generate a negative and significant coefficient were those Wealth-Rich Income-Poor households, who are the least upwardly mobile, though their stock of assets may permit them to avoid the material and health impacts associated with poverty for a long period of time.

The evidence from the analysis of the UKHLS demonstrates that it is the characteristic of household that determines their experience of living in extreme poverty. Specific household characteristics are more likely to result in a household entering into and remaining within the bottom decile making the experience of extreme poverty a long-term reality. It is structurally driven with the characteristics of the household, its typology, being the causal mechanism for this poverty. Inadequate benefit levels or lack of entitlement to benefits all contribute to this experience of extreme poverty and is particularly apparent for pensioners, carers, students, self-employed and lone parent households. Where benefit levels are higher and entitlement less restrictive households or work can be undertaken by household members, these households can escape the worst levels of poverty. The experience of households facing low wage rates or limited hours of employment, households in receipt of disability benefits and households suffering from unemployment are all less likely to remain in persistent extreme income poverty.

A UK phenomenon?

What welfare policy responses can government make in response to findings such as these? First, government can increase the resources it devotes to the elimination of poverty in general and extreme poverty in particular. Second, it can focus its attention on those specific forms of extreme poverty that cause the most concern. It may also be possible to consider solutions that are UK wide or it may be feasible to consider welfare solutions at the regional or at the level of the devolved nations. In order to consider a more localised approach through the institutions of the devolved nations and regional administrations, it is necessary to consider if the existence of extreme poverty has any specific geographical variation. The UKHLS allows for an analysis that seeks to examine whether this form of devolved and regional welfare could be expected to be more effective than that might be undertaken at a UK-wide level. Specifically, the data allows us to testing if there statistically significant differences between nations and regions in terms of how serious are the bottom decile problems for our household broad categories?

Table 3.5(A–C) presents a summary of these results. The current framework for devolution within the UK allows a focus on those nations and regions where significant devolution exists (Scotland, Wales, N Ireland and London) or is evolving (the North-West of England). For the models presented in **Tables 3.2–Table 3.4**, which examine existence in the bottom decile, entry into and exit from the bottom decile respectively, additional regression analysis is run with the

TABLE 3.5A Geographic Relationship with Household's Current Bottom Decile Status

	Scotland	*Wales*	*N. Ireland*	*North West*	*London*
Geographic dummy	Pos				
Interact Geographic dummy with…					
Pensioners			Neg	Pos*	
Carers					Pos
Rubbish Job					
Disability Benefits					
Student			Pos		
Self-employed			Pos		
Single Parent					Neg
Wealth Rich Income Poor					
Unemployment					

Source: **Table 3.2** Augmentation by Geography Current Bottom Decile Status (as of Wave B).

Note: "Neg" refers to negatively correlated at the 5% level and "Pos" refers to positively correlated.

* Indicates significance at only the 10% level (5% significance otherwise).

addition of a single geographical dummy and interaction terms between that single geographical variable and the nine broad household typology variables. Thus, given that the focus is on five geographical areas, there are five new sets of results of **Tables 3.2–Table 3.4** models. An interaction term allows for the evidence of a link between a household typology and a geographic influence to be detected. **Table 3.5(A–C)** summarises the sign and significance of the geographic dummies and interaction terms for our fifteen new specifications. A blank cell in **Table 3.5(A–C)** indicates that the geographic dummy or interaction term is insignificant; "Neg" suggests a negative and statistically significant correlation at the 5% level meaning these households' characteristic is statistically significantly correlated with its position in the bottom income decile while "Pos" indicates a

TABLE 3.5B Geographic Relationship with Entry into Bottom Decile Status

	Scotland	*Wales*	*N. Ireland*	*North West*	*London*
Geographic dummy					
Interact Geographic dummy with…					
Pensioners					
Carers		Neg*			
Rubbish Job					
Disability Benefits					
Student		Pos			Neg
Self-employed	Neg				
Single Parent		Pos		Neg*	Neg
Wealth Rich Income Poor					
Unemployment				Pos*	

Source: **Table 3.3** Augmentation by Geography Entry into Bottom Decile Status (Wave A to Wave B)

Note: "Neg" refers to negatively correlated at the 5% level and "Pos" refers to positively correlated.

* Indicates significance at only the 10% level (5% significance otherwise).

TABLE 3.5C Geographic Relationship with Exit from Wave B Bottom Decile Status (Wave B to Waves C, D, E)

	Scotland	*Wales*	*N. Ireland*	*North West*	*London*
Geographic dummy			Neg	Neg*	Pos
Interact Geographic dummy with…					
Pensioners					
Carers					
Rubbish Job					
Disability Benefits			Pos		Neg*
Student				Neg*	Pos *
Self-employed					
Single Parent					
Wealth Rich Income Poor		Pos	Neg*		
Unemployment		Neg*		Pos	

Source: **Table 3.4** Augmentation by Geography Exit from Wave B Bottom Decile Status (Wave B to Waves C, D, E).

Note: "Neg" refers to negatively correlated at the 5% level and "Pos" refers to positively correlated.

* Indicates significance at only the 10% level (5% significance otherwise).

statistically significant correlation meaning the household's outcome is less likely to be in the bottom decile with this typology. An '*' indicates that significance is found at only the 10% level. Once again, the attention below is on the presence of highly significant coefficients at the 5% level.

Table 3.5(A–C) covers a total of 15 national and region dummy coefficients and 135 interaction term coefficients (9 household types × 5 geographic areas × 3 analyses) of which 16 (12.67%) have a significant coefficient at the 5% level (10 positives, 6 negatives). **Table 3.5A** repeats the analysis covered by **Table 3.2** through adding a geographic interaction term. **Table 3.5A** shows negative and significant variables indicating that there is a statistically significant relationship between being in the lowest income decile and household typology for pensioners in the north of Ireland and single parents in London. The positive and significant results for students and the self-employed in North of Ireland and carers in London indicate these areas are less likely to have these household types in the lowest-income decile.

Table 3.5B similarly replicating **Table 3.3** examines entry into the bottom decile with a geographic interaction term and shows that a statistically negative coefficient is evident for the self-employed in Scotland and students and single parents in London indicating that acquiring these characteristics is associated with moving into the bottom decline. Positive and significant results for households less likely to move into the bottom income decile on acquiring specific household characteristics is evident for students and single parents in Wales.

Our final **Table 3.5C** highlights ability to exit the lowest income decile for households and replicates **Table 3.4**. The only positive and significant results, suggesting that extreme poverty is more transient can be identified with wealth rich but income poor in Wales, receipt of Disability benefits in the north of Ireland and unemployment in the North West of England. We find no statistically significant negative relationships, meaning no household typologies can be identified as being less likely to escape extreme poverty over time due to their geographic location.

In general, no clear single pattern of change can be identified in these results.[9] The collection of just six negative and significant coefficients suggests that geographical differences do not play a strongly statistically significant part in determining the existence, causes and duration of extreme poverty, and therefore, we can conclude that the drivers of extreme poverty are primarily UK-wide relationships without strongly identifiable geographic determinants.

Despite this overall result of homogeneity, the devolved and regional results do offer a couple of interesting points of note. First, the positive and significant variable for Scotland in the first row of **Table 3.5A** suggests that Scottish households are significantly less likely to find themselves in the bottom decile than households elsewhere in the UK. Second, extreme poverty is also evident as a particular problem for single-parent households in London, where they are significantly more likely to be the bottom decile (**Table 3.5A**), and enters into the bottom decile in becoming a single-parent household (**Table 3.5B**) and shows no evidence of being more likely to leave the bottom decile (**Table 3.5C**) over time.

In Chapter 5, the devolution of welfare policy is the subject of a more extended analysis to examine to what extent can more geographically targeted use of welfare resources provide better outcomes for low-income households and address wider questions of inequality.

Conclusion and policy implications

This chapter examined the extent to which a 'deserving' and 'undeserving' poor could be distinguished as a means to understand extreme poverty. Welfare policy since the 1980s has strongly focused upon individual responsibility and individual failure as an explanation for poverty. The increasing emphasis upon conditionality and coercion for changing behaviour of the poor thus seeks to use welfare as a means to enforce behavioural change. Within the UKHLS it is possible to identify the section of the poor where an undeserving poor, within the lowest income decile, might be expected to be located. Extreme poverty rather than a much larger population in relative poverty was the focus as this is where individual characteristics should be most clearly identifiable in the 'un-deserving poor' literature. It is also the section of the population where the incentives for behavioural change should have the most impact.

Some household types (the unemployed, carers, students, the self-employed and those who are wealth-rich but income-poor) tend to be overly represented within the bottom decile relative to other income deciles, whereas other groups tend to be under-represented (pensioners, disabled and lone parents). Thus, the title of 'undeserving' would seem to be a function of household typology for the very poorest in the income distribution, rather than individual behaviours. The acquisition of one or more of these different household typologies is also a cause of entry into the bottom decile for these same households. In contrast accessing specific welfare benefits however meagre for those with a disability or lone parents seem adequate in preventing households moving into the very poorest levels of extreme poverty.

Not only is the cause of extreme poverty a function of household typology but also once in extreme poverty, there are strong limitations on the ability to change a household's position within the income distribution. Having access to work-related benefits means than low numbers of hours of employment, a recognised disability or being unemployed are all the most likely households' types able to leave the bottom-income decile. However, work as a route out of extreme poverty is only available for a minority of the very poorest. The 2007 Great Financial Crisis, unlike other economic depressions, did not have the marked reduction in UK employment that had been a feature of early economic crises. Thus, employment rates remained high, even if wage rates stagnated and fell. In-work benefits and tax credits then provided those in employment with income to raise them out of extreme poverty (Roberts, 2016, pp. 148–152). For those households not accessing in-work benefits, even higher levels of participation in employment was not sufficient to ensure these households could escape extreme poverty. The results of the UKHLS suggests that segmentation of the low paid workforce gives rise to very different outcomes.

Unemployment within this group was linked more strongly with frictional rather than structural forms of unemployment. Similarly, disability provides a means to exit the bottom decile, for those able to be deemed sufficiently disabled to fail the Work Capability Assessment at least. In conclusion, we can suggest that for those accessing in-work benefits, exit from the lowest income decile could be observed. However, for those unable to access in-work benefits, existence within the lowest income decile was much more prevalent.

For other groups, however, the picture is far bleaker. For carers, students, the self-employed and those who are reliant upon their savings, there is no evidence to suggest their household typology acts to support their exit from extreme poverty. Carers as a particularly disadvantaged group, face long-term extreme poverty by taking on a social role in the care of others. Self-employment is also a route into extreme poverty for many households from which there is often little hope of escape. Single parents are not disproportionately likely to be in the bottom decile, but if they do enter, the bottom decile is generally unsuccessful in exiting their circumstances.

Finally, in most cases, there appears to be little geographical differences with these patterns of extreme poverty as it is generated from a UK-wide set of welfare policies designed to largely exclude specific households from the support needed. Work as a route out of poverty may perhaps be more accurately re-defined as 'work or starve'.

The evidence from this chapter identifies inadequate support for the extreme poor found in the poorest 10% of households within the UK. Specific households may be able to access welfare support lifting them from the worst forms of extreme income poverty while others remain vulnerable to long-term deprivation. This does not fit with the framework of a deserving and undeserving poor in modern British society. Instead, it suggests structural features of extreme poverty in which the benefit system systematically deprives households of a means to live in anything other than the most deprived conditions.

We can conclude that the existence of extreme poverty, its duration and those forced to endure its effects derive primarily from a socially constructed structural environment rather than individual choice. Conceptualisation of a 'deserving' and 'undeserving' poor fits the patterns of extreme poverty poorly in the UKHLS dataset.

Appendix 3

TABLE A3.1 Bottom Decile Household Typologies in UK Household Longitudinal Study (UKHLS) 2010–2014

	UK Household Longitudinal Survey UKHLS 2010–2014					
*Household Typology**	*Wave A*	*Wave B*	*Wave C*	*Wave D*	*Wave E*	*Average of A–E*
Lone pensioner households**						
- no pension at all	1.0%	0.8%	0.6%	0.4%	0.3%	0.6%
- not claiming State Pension	2.9%	0.9%	0.9%	0.8%	0.6%	1.2%
- State Pension is the only pension claimed	5.9%	6.5%	5.7%	6.2%	5.8%	6.0%
- State Pension and Pension Credits only	0.4%	1.1%	1.3%	1.2%	1.9%	1.2%
- other lone pensioners	6.3%	7.5%	6.7%	7.3%	7.0%	7.0%
Pensioner couple households**						
- no pension at all	0.1%	0.1%	0.0%	0.1%	0.1%	0.1%
- not claiming State Pension	0.7%	0.2%	0.0%	0.0%	0.0%	0.2%
- State Pension is the only pension claimed	1.9%	2.3%	2.0%	2.0%	2.3%	2.1%
- State Pension and Pension Credits only	0.2%	0.1%	0.3%	0.3%	0.4%	0.3%
- other pensioner couples	2.0%	3.2%	2.8%	2.7%	3.1%	2.8%
Households including carer(s)						
- one adult household	3.4%	4.7%	4.4%	3.8%	4.0%	4.1%
- multiple adult household	17.6%	16.7%	17.4%	17.3%	16.0%	17.0%
Households with low wage rates and/or limited hours						
- 22–64-year-old earning less than the minimum wage	7.0%	9.1%	10.5%	11.4%	12.4%	10.1%
- 18–21-year-old earning less than the minimum wage	0.3%	0.3%	0.3%	0.5%	0.4%	0.4%

(Continued)

TABLE A3.1 Bottom Decile Household Typologies in UK Household Longitudinal Survey (UKHLS) 2010–2014 (*Continued*)

	UK Household Longitudinal Survey UKHLS 2010–2014					
*Household Typology**	*Wave A*	*Wave B*	*Wave C*	*Wave D*	*Wave E*	*Average of A–E*
- 16–17-year-old earning less than the minimum wage	0.1%	0.0%	0.1%	0.1%	5.9%	1.2%
- 16–64-year-old earning less than the living wage	10.6%	4.4%	5.8%	6.0%	0.8%	5.5%
- 1–15 hours of work	2.3%	1.0%	1.0%	0.9%	3.0%	1.6%
- 16–31 hours of work	6.4%	3.3%	3.7%	2.9%	3.2%	3.9%
Households with disability benefit recipient(s)						
- one adult household	2.8%	3.5%	2.4%	2.3%	3.3%	2.9%
- multiple adult household	5.2%	6.9%	6.8%	6.8%	6.0%	6.3%
Households with pupils/ students (16 and over)						
- one adult household	4.1%	4.2%	3.7%	4.0%	4.0%	4.0%
- multiple adult household	14.6%	13.0%	11.7%	12.1%	12.6%	12.8%
Households with self-employed						
- one adult household	3.8%	3.9%	4.1%	4.0%	4.4%	4.0%
- multiple adult household	9.4%	13.1%	12.8%	13.3%	13.3%	12.4%
Lone parent households						
- no transfer income	1.2%	0.9%	0.9%	0.9%	0.5%	0.9%
- has transfer income	0.1%	0.1%	0.2%	0.1%	0.1%	0.1%
Wealth rich, income poor***	6.3%	5.8%	5.7%	7.1%	4.8%	5.9%
Households with unemployed adults						
- one adult (no unemployment type benefits)	5.7%	4.7%	3.7%	4.0%	3.7%	4.4%
- one adult (with unemployment type benefits)	2.9%	2.8%	3.2%	2.8%	3.5%	3.0%
- multiple unemployed adults (no unemp. type benefits)	9.4%	9.2%	9.2%	9.3%	8.2%	9.1%
- multiple unemployed adults (with unemp. type benefits)	4.0%	4.7%	5.0%	4.9%	4.2%	4.6%
Lone occupant (no explanation for decile one status)	6.2%	4.4%	4.4%	4.4%	5.4%	5.0%
Multiple occupants (no explanation for decile one status)	4.6%	3.4%	3.2%	3.8%	3.0%	3.6%
Total	**149.4%**	**142.8%**	**140.5%**	**143.7%**	**144.2%**	**144.3%**

Source: UK Household Longitudinal Survey, Waves A–E covering the period 2010–2014.

* This table does not treat household categories as being mutually exclusive, and so the final column shows that the percentages aggregate to 144.3%, i.e. more than 100%. Thus, a household with pensioner who is a carer for another individual is classified as *both* a pensioner *and* a carer.

** Retired people not in receipt of a pension are classified as pensioners in the UKHLS.

*** Wealth rich, income poor is chosen, by the authors, to be households in which investment income is greater than 17% of all household income and therefore have significant wealth.

TABLE A3.2 Logistic Regression for being in the Bottom Decile in Wave B (33 Household Scenarios)

Logistic Regression	Number of obs = 27,157
	LR chi^2(37) = 3899.28
	Prob > chi^2 = 0.0000
Log likelihood = −6852.9038	Pseudo R^2 = 0.2215

	UK Household Longitudinal Survey UKHLS 2010					
*Household Typology**	*Coefficient*	*Standard Error*	*z*	*P> |z|*	*95% Confidence*	*Interval*
Lone pensioner households**						
- no pension at all	−.6255099	.3462758	−1.81	0.071	−1.304198	.0531781
- not claiming State Pension	.0901609	.2341501	0.39	0.700	−0.368765	.5490868
- State Pension is the only pension claimed	−.6593684	.097864	−6.74	0.000	−0.851178	−.4675585
- State Pension and Pension Credits only	.7873553	.2039447	3.86	0.000	0.387631	1.18708
- other lone pensioners	1.017269	.0844219	12.05	0.000	0.851805	1.18273
Pensioner couple households**						
- no pension at all	−1.023623	1.030989	−0.99	0.321	−3.044324	.9970785
- not claiming State Pension	−.5505358	.4823746	−1.14	0.254	−1.495973	.3949009
- State Pension is the only pension claimed	−.7303515	.1571571	−4.65	0.000	−1.038374	−.4223293
- State Pension and Pension Credits only	1.994979	.7175852	2.78	0.005	0.588538	3.40142
- other pensioner couples	1.520876	.1192008	12.76	0.000	1.287247	1.754505
Households including carer(s)						
- one adult household	−2.053899	.1439942	−14.26	0.000	−2.336123	−1.771676
- multiple adult household	−.6563435	.0655891	−10.01	0.000	−0.784896	−.5277912
Households with low wage rates and/or limited hours						
- 22–64-year-old earning less than the minimum wage	−.6201419	.1213132	−5.11	0.000	−0.857911	−.3823725
- 18–21-year-old earning less than the minimum wage	−.5474317	.3737861	−1.46	0.143	−1.280039	.1851756
- 16–17-year-old earning less than the minimum wage	.3650345	1.044215	0.35	0.727	−1.681589	2.411658
- 16–64-year-old earning less than the living wage	−.9135536	.1127822	−8.10	0.000	−1.134603	−.6925045
- 1–15 hours of work	.0662495	.0033386	19.84	0.000	0.059706	.0727931
- 16–31 hours of work	−.0002058	.0000415	−4.96	0.000	−0.000287	−.0001245

(*Continued*)

TABLE A3.2 Logistic Regression for being in the Bottom Decile in Wave B (33 Household Scenarios) (*Continued*)

Logistic Regression	Number of obs = 27,157					
	LR chi²(37) = 3899.28					
	Prob > chi² = 0.0000					
Log likelihood = −6852.9038	Pseudo R^2 = 0.2215					
	UK Household Longitudinal Survey UKHLS 2010					
*Household Typology**	*Coefficient*	*Standard Error*	*z*	*P* > |*z*|	*95% Confidence*	*Interval*
Households with disability benefit recipient(s)						
- one adult household	.9534473	.1192375	8.00	0.000	0.7197461	1.187149
- multiple adult household	.8185991	.0865419	9.46	0.000	0.6489801	.988218
Households with pupils/students (16 and over)						
- one adult household	−1.805234	.1480162	−12.20	0.000	−2.09534	−1.515127
- multiple adult household	−.411964	.0703214	−5.86	0.000	−.5497914	−.2741367
Households with self-employed						
- one adult household	−.6394 704	.1233026	−5.19	0.000	−.881139	−.3978019
- multiple adult household	.0305425	.0682912	0.45	0.655	−.1033058	.1643907
Lone parent households						
- no transfer income	1.312687	.2410763	5.45	0.000	.8401865	1.785188
- has transfer income	2.979744	.7311623	4.08	0.000	1.546693	4.412796
Wealth rich, income poor***	−.4602577	.0989537	−4.65	0.000	−.6542034	−.266312
Households with unemployed adults						
- one adult (no unemployment type benefits)	−1.96048	.1418517	−13.82	0.000	−2.238504	−1.682456
- one adult (with unemployment type benefits)	−1.807446	.1765768	−10.24	0.000	−2.15353	−1.461362
- multiple unemployed adults (no unemp. type benefits)	−.9047325	.0844034	−10.72	0.000	−1.07016	−.7393049
- multiple unemployed adults (with unemp. type benefits)	−.719916	.1123993	−6.40	0.000	−.9402145	−.4996174
Constant	85.29759	21.81025	3.91	0.000	42.55028	128.0449

Source: UK Household Longitudinal Survey, Waves A (2010).

* Retired people not in receipt of a pension are classified as pensioners in the UKHLS.

** *Wealth rich, income poor is chosen, by the authors, to be households in which investment income is greater than 17% of all household income and therefore have significant wealth.*

Notes

1 The McClements Scale (1977) provides a mechanism for modifying raw household income data to reflect the effect of a household's composition (i.e. the number and type of household members) on the standard of living that can be expected to be achieved from that level of income. For further information, see Chapter 2 and McClements (1977).
2 See Chapter 2, for details of the derivation of the equivalised monthly household income variable net of housing costs eNHMI.
3 Control variables are used to ensure the variable being tested (household typology) is not biased by a non-observed characteristic. The six control variables are the regional labour force participation rate (and its square), the regional public sector share of employment (and its square), a dummy variable for the household living in an urban area and a dummy variable for the household needing a language translator.
4 A feature of the bottom decile is that some households report negative after housing costs income (see Chapter 2). Again, this could be a feature of the relying upon savings for income, low levels of work for the self-employment or households avoiding taxation by diverting income into dividends.
5 There is insufficient inter-temporal variability in some of these 33 household scenarios to permit regression analysis of the dynamics of bottom decile status over time – statistical software (such as the Stata package that we use) will insist on dropping such low variability variables to avoid problems of multicollinearity. Rather than relying on the default, mechanical solution of a statistical package this analysis reduces the dimensionality of the problem in the remaining statistical analyses by the use of the 9 broad categories noted above (pensioners, carers, etc.).
6 Since the analysis focuses on entry into the bottom decile, rather than continued presence in that bottom decile, we exclude from our sample households that were, as of Wave A, already in the bottom decile.
7 To be consistent with **Table 3.2**, six control variables were also included to exclude non-household specific effects from the analysis. These are the regional labour force participation rate (and its square), the regional public sector share of employment (and its square), a dummy variable for the household living in an urban area and a dummy variable for the household needing a language translator.
8 For consistency with the earlier results, an ordered logit regression was also run with the dependent variable is an (0,1,2) ordered variable where 0 represents households in the bottom decile for equivalised net monthly income, 1 represents households in deciles two and three, and 2 represents households in deciles four to ten. These ordered logit results were again consistent with the logit results presented here and as a result this alternative modelling strategy is not considered further.
9 Regressing a dependent variable on a set of purely random variables would expect 2.5% of those variables to generate positive and significant coefficients, and 2.5% to generate negative and significant coefficients; thus, for a set of 150 coefficients we would expect 3.75 (i.e. 2.5% of 150) negative and significant coefficients purely by chance.

References

Aldridge, H., Parekh, A., MacInnes, T. and Kenway, P. (2011), *Monitoring Poverty and Social Exclusion 2011*, York: Joseph Rowntree Trust.

Barnet, C. (1986), *The Audit of War*, London: MacMillan.

Barr, N and Coulter, F. (1990), Social Security: Solution or Problem?, in N. Barr and J. Hills (eds.), *The State of Welfare: The Welfare State in Britain Since 1974*, Oxford: Clarendon Press, pp. 328–329.

Bertram, C. and Wright, S. (2012), 'Working Scotland', in G. Mooney and G. Scott (eds.), *Social Justice and Social Policy in Scotland*, Bristol: Policy Press, pp. 203–238.

Child Poverty Action Group, (2003), *Welfare Benefits and Tax Credits Handbook*, London: CPAG.

Choonara, J. (2019), *Insecurity, Precarious Work and Labour Markets: Challenging the Orthodoxy*, London: Palgrave Macmillan.

Department for Work and Pensions. (2006), *A New Deal for Welfare: Empowering People to Work*, London; HMSO: Consultation Report.

Department for Work and Pensions. (2018), https://www.gov.uk/employment-support-allowance accessed 12th January 2018.

Dilnot, A. (1995). The Assessment: The Future of the Welfare State. *Oxford Review of Economic Policy* 1(3), pp. 1–10.

Dilnot, A., Kay, J. and Morris, C. (1984), *The Reform of Social Security*, Oxford: Clarendon Press.

Doogan, K. (2009), *New Capitalism? The Transformation of Work*, Cambridge: Polity Press.

Dorling, D. (2010), *Injustice: Why Social Inequality Persists*, London: Pluto Press.

Fletcher, D. and Wright, S. (2018). A Hand Up or a Slap Down? Criminalising Benefit Claimants in Britain via Strategies of Surveillance, Sanctions and deterrence. *Critical Social Policy*, 38(2), pp. 323–344.

Fraser, D. (1989), *The Evolution of the Welfare State* (2nd edition), London, MacMillan.

Goodman, C. and Danson, M. (eds.) (2019), *Exploring Basic Income in Scotland*, Scotland: Citizens Basic Income Network.

Guardian. (2011a), David Starkey Claims 'The Whites Have Become Black', 13th August 2011, available at http://www.theguardian.com/uk/2011/aug/13/david-starkey-claims-whites-black.

Guardian. (2011b), https://www.theguardian.com/media/2011/aug/15/david-starkey-newsinght-race-remarks

Jones, J. (2011), August 2011: A Riot of Our Own. International Socialism Journal 132, p. 52.

Lewis, P., Taylor, M. and Ball, J. (2011), *Clarke Blames English Riots on a 'Broken Penal System'*, The Guardian, Monday, 5 September.

McClements, L.D. (1977), Equivalence Scales for Children. *Journal of Public Economics* 8, pp. 191–210.

Office of National Statistics. (2015), *EMP09: Employees and Self-Employed by Occupation,* 13th May 2015, available at https://www.ons.gov.uk/search?q=emp09 accessed 15th June 2015.

Office for National Statistics. (2019), *EMP16: Underemployment and Overemployment of Those Aged 16 and Over*, London. available at: https://www.ons.gov.uk/employmentandlabourmarket/peopleinwork/employmentandemployeetypes/datasets/underemploymentandoveremploymentemp16/current.

Palmer, G., MacInnes, T. and Kenway, P. (2008), *Monitoring Poverty and Social Exclusion 2008*, York: Joseph Rowntree Trust.

Roberts, M. (2016), *The Long Depression: How It Happened, Why It Happened and What Happens Next, Chicago: USA, Haymarket Books.*

Standing, G. (2011), *The Precariat: The New Dangerous Class*, London: Bloomsbury Academic.

Thompson, P., Winfield, H., Simmons, D. and Linney, J. (2003), *Paying for Care Handbook: A Guide to Services, Charges and Welfare Benefits for Adults in Need of Care in the Community or in Care Homes* (4th edition), London: CPAG.

Tinson, A., Ayrton, C., Barker, K., Barry Born, T., Aldridge, H. and Kenway, P. (2016), *Monitoring Poverty and Social Exclusion 2016*, York: Joseph Rowntree Trust.

Townsend, P. and Davidson, N. (1992), *Inequalities in Health*, London: Penguin.

UNISON (2013), The Living Wage, http://www.unison.org.uk/our-campaigns/unison-campaigns/a-living-wage/home/ accessed 14th October 2014.

UK Government (1995), *Jobseekers Act 1995*, London: HMSO.

Wacquant, L. (2009), *Punishing the Poor: The Neoliberal Government of Social Insecurity*, Durham, NC: Duke University Press.

Wilkinson, R. and Pickett, K. (2009), *The Spirit Level: Why More Equal Societies Almost Always Do Better*, London: Allen Lane.

Wills, J. (2009). Subcontracted Employment and Its Challenge to Labor. *Labor Studies Journal* 34(4), pp. 441–460.

4

THE TOP 10%

Income and wealth inequality

Introduction

In Chapter 3, we demonstrated how the use of the UK Household Longitudinal Study (UKHLS), Understanding Society, could be utilised to examine the characteristics of households in extreme poverty and test for the validity of the policy discourse around a deserving and underserving poor. The evidence derived from the data demonstrated the structural nature of extreme poverty in which specific household characteristics not only increase the likelihood of a household falling into the lowest 10% of the income distribution but also ensure the household's ability to escape extreme poverty is severely curtailed. The conclusion drawn from these findings was that extreme poverty is a socially constructed structural phenomenon within the UK, developed through specific ideologies aimed at creating an 'undeserving' pool of extreme poverty. Poverty and inequality are therefore not simply due to differences in human decision-making but instead linked to structural features of the UK economy whose influence differentially impacts upon those at the bottom of the income distribution. However, it is not sufficient just to locate the existence of extreme poverty as structural poverty when examining inequality. We have to be able to examine the extent of similar structural inequalities existing elsewhere within the income distribution, and in particular in the area of extreme wealth for the highest income households.

The extent of poverty and inequality then is a social decision in any society and those at the bottom of the income distribution are required to suffer the consequences for this decision-making while those at the top benefit from these social decisions. Thus, while the conclusion drawn from this approach is to suggest that government has an important role to play in the creation and implementation of redistributive policies, there is also a need to examine the extent to which redistribution is feasible within the income distribution. In order to

DOI: 10.4324/9781315179957-4

demonstrate the potentiality of redistribution, we require an understanding of not simply those at the bottom of the income distribution but also those at the top.

In this chapter, we seek to follow the approach adopted in Chapter 3, where we examined the characteristics of those in the bottom decile and moved onto test for causation in the creation of extreme poverty. Here, we address the top 10% of the income distribution. Similarly, we seek to test the extent to which the top decile of the income distribution can be understood to be a separate social grouping distinct from the rest of the nine deciles? Since our expectation is that there are distinct social and economic differences between the top decile and the rest of the income distribution, we also wish to examine whether these differences are linked to the likelihood of households remaining within the top 10% of households. Thus again, we are interested in the process of mobility leading to causation as well as correlation. While the top 10% of households in the income distribution may have distinct characteristics, our knowledge of the growth of wealth as well as income inequality may also result in further stratification within even these high-income households. As a result, we examine not only the top 10% but the top 1% of households in the income distribution for these characteristics.

Before addressing these questions, it is necessary to take an anthropological digression and return to our discussion of inequality, its origins and development touched on in Chapter 1.

Before inequality

The anthropological and historical records suggest that the marked changes in the development of human societies are such that neither poverty nor inequality can be regarded as an ahistorical state of human existence (Flannery and Marcus, 2012). Anthropologists have uncovered evidence from a wide range of early human artefacts which indicate that early societies were most likely characterised by mutuality, co-operation and sharing such that they are described as affluent and egalitarian. There appears to be little evidence for the existence of homo-economicus; in which human behaviour is typified by economics of individualised utility maximisation and decision-making. Rather than early human history being characterised by a naked unmediated economic life of pseudo-Darwinian brutality, near starvation, theft and war, in which the weak fell by the wayside as the strong rose to dominate, the historical evidence suggests something very different, and more complex. To make this point is not to idealise early human existence but to recognise that these societies sustainability could only be achieved through the mutuality and cooperation of all participants (Raworth, 2017). This evidence provides us with a recognition of the primacy of the historical context for an understanding of the poverty and inequality in contemporary capitalism.

The vast majority of human history, accounting for around the first 137,000 of the 150,000 years since modern humans can be identified as emerging as a species, is one of small foraging and hunter-gather groups of no more than perhaps 30 to 40 individuals. These early societies were not ones in which poverty can be recognised.

Poverty, we may suggest, is an inability to generate sufficient resources for a population's needs within the set of permissible possibilities in any given productive system. Certainly, scarcity existed within early hunter-gatherer societies with evidence of groups periodically resorting to looting, or warfare, when scarcity prevailed. However, Shalin's (1988) study, *Stone-Age Economics*, makes the distinction that these early hunter-gather societies while being materially poor were not 'in poverty'. Indeed, the extent to which these societies were sustainable with much higher levels of leisure time available after immediate needs were satisfied, leads to the suggestion that these societies were the first 'affluent' societies (Cook, 1974; Shalin, 1988). While we do not have to go so far as to suggest these societies constitute the first affluent societies, we can suggest that scarcity or warfare were neither a continuous nor the most prevalent features of these societies. Warfare is a potentially high-risk economic strategy to adopt for such fragile groups where the loss of even one or two individuals could threaten the survival of the whole group. Even more so, societies which were persistently warlike could only have been sustainable if they had access to other less warlike and more productive societies. These more productive societies must then have been sufficiently productive to, not only be internally sustainable but productive enough to be able to suffer losses from warfare.

Nomadic hunter-gather or foraging societies demonstrate tool production primarily for productive labour rather than warfare. Further, these societies were capable of producing cultural artefacts in cave paintings, sculpted figures and symbolic totems and customs. Thus, they required time to labour which was not focused upon production of food and shelter or warfare and yet their labour must have been sufficient to produce quantities of food and shelter to be sustainable over time. Hunter-gatherer societies may have been small, of limited resources, prone to crisis and disease but these were features of the extent of human economic development and not one of social organisation or human nature.

Within the productive constraints of the period, covering the vast majority of human existence, poverty cannot be identified. Indeed, the anthropological evidence suggests that sustainability is the common feature of most of human existence. Again Eric Roll makes the point that observability of effort and satisfaction makes both exploitative relationships impossible and unnecessary and thus '... there is no need for any elaborate social or economic theory' (Roll, 1953, p. 22).

If poverty is not a readily identifiable feature of these societies, then can we suggest that neither is inequality? Private property is suggested to exist, as found in burial sites, but it cannot be identified with wider social or institutional hierarchy. All important economic aspects of life, land and food resources were collectively controlled and collective labour involving all members of the society was required to hunt and gather food (Burke-Leacock, 2008, p. 101). Indeed, the very fragility of these small societies is the explanation for a belief that these were based upon high levels of mutuality and cooperation. Childe (1965, pp. 46–53) identifies the egalitarian nature of these societies through their collaborative labours in food production, the existence of co-operative trade and exchange between coastal and inland communities through the widespread movement of sea-fish to inland communities and the communal identification of institutions through loose or fictional 'kinship' rather than hereditary connections. Early forms of sea-based trade networks, including inter-island networks stretching across some hundreds of kilometres, appear to be taking place as early as 20,000 years ago in Western Melanesia, New Guinea, (Kirkch, 1991, p. 146). However, equally importantly while authority and leadership are identified, it is suggested to emerge through age, expertise and prestige and is, noticeably, not clearly singularly gendered or hereditary. Thus, specialist traders with navigation skills appear to be important in the development of trade within the Western Melanesia trade routes (ibid, p. 156). In the case of the agricultural peoples of the highlands of New Guinea Golson and Gardner suggest that 'the pre-eminence of individuals and the fortunes of groups, whether tied to magical or ritual virtuosity, ceremonial exchange or marital success, never produced conditions that could guarantee their intergenerational transmission' (Golson and Gardner, 1990, p. 397). The archaeological evidence indicates that the majority of human existence is one in which poverty and inequality were not natural tendencies, perpetual or structural features.

It is not until around 13,000 years ago that we can identify settled communities of one hundred or more individuals, known as the Mesolithic or middle stone-age, and less than 10,000 years ago that the agricultural developments classified in what is described as the first agricultural revolution (Harman, 1999, pp. 3–16). The development of settled agricultural societies, first with the organised clearing of ground and sowing of seeds and later with the development of irrigation and some 7,000 years ago evidence of ploughing, raised the potential for the production of food and the creation of surpluses. It is these surpluses within settled agriculturalist communities that anthropologists identify with the development of the first civilisations characterised by the rise of organised culture, customs being codified into religious beliefs and formal hierarchical social structures. These hierarchies include, eventually, institutionalised subordination of women emerging for the first time in human history (ibid, pp. 18–19).

Alongside these developments, emerge the first examples of poverty and inequality. The ability to generate surpluses through organised agricultural labour processes permits the emergence of control over the ownership and use of both the labour generating surpluses and the surpluses themselves. Characteristic of these hierarchical societies is the development of Deities, gods and organised worship identified by our earliest examples of temples and places of worship. It is then only then, from approximately 3,000 B.C, that we can identify common features of the structure of modern human societies first emerging; social hierarchy and stratification and alongside it the emergence of inequality and poverty. By 1170 B.C., we also find evidence for the first recorded strike in human history, by pyramid builders, as conflict over inequality and poverty becomes identifiable and the first knowledge of slavery or 'unfree' labour in De Ste Croix's (Harman, 1999, p. 37) terminology. The surpluses derived from this unfree labour also permits the development of a controlling privileged layer within these societies. De Ste Croix's study of the ancient Greek world highlights the importance of unfree labour for the development and continuities of these ruling classes and its widespread occurrence across the Mediterranean and Asian economies, but only, it should be noted, as far back as 400 B.C. (De Ste Croix, 1981, pp. 133–174 and Appendix 2).

It should be stressed that although these features first emerge, they are neither uniform nor continuous in human societies. These class-based civilisations are themselves prone to crisis, warfare and collapse, as were the earlier egalitarian-based hunter-gather and foraging societies that preceded them. Similarly, hunter-gather or foraging societies continued in large parts of the world where settled agricultural production was neither necessary for survival nor indeed viable. It is precisely the continuation of these forms of societies that has permitted contemporary anthropologists to make many of the inferences about human development briefly outlined above.

The discussion over early human societies' economic and social structures and the later emergence of poverty and inequality pre-dates the era when influence over the environment had lasting effects on the world's ecology that is now identified with the modern Anthropocene era (Angus, 2016). However, leap forward to the Anthropocene era of the twenty-first century and advanced capitalist market-based societies allows us to identify marked changes in the underlying theories behind the development of inequality. An evolutionary economic approach sympathetic to the outcomes of capitalist development would suggest inequality, and consequently, poverty is an inevitable initial result of progressive development due to innovation (McCloskey, 2017). However, subsequent moves towards increasing equality emerge over time due to the dispersion of technological innovation and a general process of convergence both between and within economies. A 'Kuznets' curve exists in which an initial increase of inequality is reversed over time with economic progress via the diffusion of the benefits of economic development (Kuznets, 1955). Debates over the extent of inequality within a largely neo-classical literature, therefore, identifies the impediments to these market-based economic processes that prolong and deepen inequality of outcomes. Within an institutionalist economic school of thought North (1991) and Olson (1971) together represent many of the contemporary ideas underpinning this approach. North's work identifies the role of defined property rights and institutional structures maximising the role for market exchange and market information in the development of economic growth. Government acting to establish market mechanisms for the efficient allocation of resources through the price mechanism ensures equality of outcome. Olson similarly provides a property rights-based explanation for the failures of economies to continue to grow, and indeed even decline. Tendencies towards sclerotic decline, brought about by the growth of rent-seeking redistributive coalitions, impede market information leading to inefficiencies in resource allocation (Olson, 1982). Thus, interest groups emerging over time create the coalitions capable of diverting the efficient distribution of wealth within an economy. These distributional coalitions are then essentially understood as crowding-out good opportunities for new innovatory investment and this then leads to lower growth and economic decline. Olson (1982) identifies defeat in war, revolution and military occupation as means by which these distributional coalitions are swept away while Schumpter (1994), within a similar disruptive crisis-focused vein, emphasises the role of 'creative destruction'. Schumpeter locates the role played by innovation in the creation of new industries which sweep away older, less efficient, forms of production within a revolutionary transformation within economies. In both cases, market-based incentives return as the primary focus of attention in economic, utility and profit maximising decision-making. Less catastrophically evolutionary economic approaches, such as Casson (2003), identify lower-level disruption through evolutionary yet innovatory managerial advance as a mechanism for these developments.

None of the above approaches necessitate the removal of the role of the state as an intermediary body within advanced capitalist society but all locate its role within a narrow, facilitating, role providing the framework for market exchange, widely referred to as the 'rules of the game' (North, 1991). Private individual market exchange with minimal development of re-distributive welfare policies, due to the negative effects of crowding-out of all state-level interventions, are therefore the idealisation form of economy within neo-classical schools of thought.

In contrast to the neo-classical approach to inequality authors, which identify market failures for the rise of inequality and its social consequences place a greater emphasis upon state intervention within economies to address deleterious impacts of externalities within markets. Private markets can externalise costs in areas where the price mechanism is either absent or too high to internalise. Thus pollution, waste and climate change lie outside of the cost structure for private markets and highlight the existence of market failures within economic development (Raworth, 2017; Meagher, 2020). This, broadly Keynesian literature, places a focus upon the developmental nature of state intervention and replacement of market signals by non-market planning and coordination for the resolution of market failures. Ranging from liberals such as Beveridge (1967) to post-Marxist Keynesians such as Varoufakis (2016) the state plays an important larger redistributive role. This redistributive role is itself aimed at generating more rapid growth to provide sustainable but higher levels of government intervention. Importantly, the state within this framework is not simply an institutional body whose role is to deal with market failure but it is an integral part of the market-based system of production. (Krugman, 1994 pp. 245–280; Elliott and Atkinson, 2016). The state acts to promote innovation, growth and wealth creation. Within this framework, active state intervention creates domestic and international frameworks whereby risk can be managed and investment, trade and growth can be encouraged. One recent example arises from Massucato (2018) who makes the case for an 'entrepreneurial state', in which the state is embedded in the resource allocation decision-making underpinning innovation and development.

Within this Keynesian framework institutional barriers to development, immobility or lack of access to resources are the means by which inequality shapes individuals lives and has a negative impact on human development. Rawls' (1985) places an emphasis upon the need for redistributive mechanisms to ensure fairness and justice can remove structural inequalities to facilitate an equality of outcomes. Sen (1995) uses a human-rights-based philosophy identifying government action to ensure an equality of opportunity, as a mechanism through which structural inequality can be minimised. The broad concept of a 'social wage' institutionalising redistributive policies within a system of social security and welfare states encapsulated these ideas within the post-Second World War settlements in the developed economies (Milward, 1992; Alcroft, 1993).

Finally, structural inequality deriving from the exploitation of human labour, underpinned by a capitalist mode of production, is the focus of attention for Marxist approaches to inequality. Callinicos (2000) considers the inevitability of inequality within an economic system in which exploitation of labour, in the creation of surplus value, is the motivation of the economy under capitalism. Both poverty and inequality are an inherent consequence of class-based production systems generally and within capitalism specifically. This is due to labour income being driven as close to the subsistence level that is required for the reproduction of labour power in the pursuit of maximising absolute levels of surplus value generated in the labour process (Marx, 1980, pp. 185–226). Competition for accumulation of surplus value, therefore, creates the necessity for exploitation of the working class and inevitable class-based conflict emerges in the negotiation over the wage rate and questions of a wider social wage (Shaikh, 2016, pp. 638–676). Without transformation of society, both poverty and inequality are maintained and indeed poverty plays an important role within capitalism. Unlike previous class societies, the construction of a 'reserve army of labour' providing the potential for the entry of new workers into production processes is a necessity to the capitalist mode of production and thus poverty and inequality are essential to the creation of surplus value under capitalist production (Marx, 1970, pp. 628–640). Within a Marxist framework, the economic divergence identified within the neo-classical school is not then a temporary inevitable phenomenon in the development of capitalism over time but the permanent product of the social class structures under capitalism. Class conflicts arising out of these structural inequalities may be directly over the wage rate paid to employed workers or over a broader defence of the social wage that emerged in the post-war Keynesian period. A Marxist understanding of anti-poverty strategies focuses on the extent to which broader social forces can bring influence to bear on decision-making institutions, governments and states. In doing so working-class struggles promote redistribution initiatives contributing to a wage rate or a collective social wage.

Elephants and patrimonial capitalism

Much of the discussion above is encapsulated in contemporary debates over the emergent patterns of inequality that have occurred from the last quarter of the twentieth century. Income has grown at a very rapid pace for those at the very top of the income distribution. At the same time, there is debate over the extent to which income convergence has occurred within the rest of the income distribution with the result that there are conflicting interpretations over the degree to which income inequality exists.

Piketty (2014) documents in his extensive study of income and wealth inequality the impact that a higher return to asset wealth (*r*) generates in contrast to lower returns to labour income through employment (*g*) (pp. 336–376). Piketty charts the initial historical reduction in concentration of wealth in the very top income decile from the early twentieth century as a property-owning 'patrimonial middle-class' emerged. This, however, went into reverse by the late twentieth-first century such that levels of wealth inequality had returned to levels not seen since the era prior to World War One. The patrimonial middle class, identified as the 40% of the population found in the four income deciles below the top income decile gained small but significant 'crumbs' from the table of the wealthiest in society such that whereas the top 10% of incomes by 1900 held over 50% of national income this had fallen by as much as half in some advanced economies by the 1970s (Piketty, 2014, p. 262). However, from the 1980s onwards into the first two decades of the twenty-first century, this process went into rapid reverse with the result that the proportion of total income claimed by the top income decile had returned to pre-World War One levels (Piketty, 2014, pp. 1–35).

Moreover, by the twenty-first century, the top decile was itself increasingly a highly stratified and fixed layer in society. While those in the 'bottom' (*sic*) nine percentiles of this highest income decile still required a majority of labour income for their position, this was an increasingly elitist layer of private sector managers and senior officials within the public sector. To be within this elitist senior managerial group, their earnings rose to levels two, three or four times the average wage. Piketty considers the changing nature of management professionalisation in the era of the second half of the twentieth century as a period in which fluidity within this group would have previously have been evident. In the middle decades of the twentieth century, a highly qualified technician in the private sector may have found themselves in, or near, the highest income decile. However, by the end of the twentieth century, only middle to higher management, often those with postgraduate qualifications such as MBAs, would now reach these levels. Similarly, in relation to qualification in the public sector while teachers, university professors and a wide range of government officials would have been firmly within this group at mid-century, by the end of the twentieth century only an elite layer of these individuals and more commonly the senior management in schools, universities and government now reached these heights

(Piketty, 2014, pp. 279–300). Thus, now the 'bottom' nine percentiles of the top income decile were increasingly identifiable as senior managers, business owners and entrepreneurs in the private sector or doctors, senior government officials or barristers in the public sector.

In contrast, however, the social composition of the very top 1% was very different from those strata below them. It has historically always been far less fluid than those immediately below and has always had much greater reliance upon income from inherited wealth and rent rather than labour for the majority of their income. Piketty further suggests dividend income rather than rent, from land, becomes the increasingly dominant form of income for this percentile in the form of financial assets, primarily stocks, shares and partnerships (2014, pp. 301–303). The highest income percentile is then characterised by an elite that emerges from, and is dominated by, the rise of financial capitalism rather than landed interests or manufacturing. For Piketty, this 1% are central to understanding the re-emergence and dominance of patrimonial capitalism.

Crucially, important to the conclusions drawn in Piketty's work is that for the rest of the income distribution, the bottom nine income deciles, the growth of income from financial wealth has been absent with the result that income inequality has grown rapidly in the twenty-first century driven by a narrow ownership of financial assets. To quote Piketty '... in the second decade of the twenty-first century, inequalities of wealth that had supposedly disappeared are close to regaining or even surpassing their historical highs' (2014, p. 471).

As would be expected Piketty's broadly Keynesian-based understanding and policy focus, identifying proposals for the taxation of financial transactions such as the Tobin Tax, has been challenged by those focusing upon both neo-classical and Marxist interpretations. McCloskey's (2017) neo-classical critique places primacy on market-based solutions of long-run growth and convergence rather than state regulation as the basis for addressing inequalities. Without state intervention, a Kuznet-style 'great moderation' will inevitably see factor mobility ensuring inequality is reduced over time. The human consequences for those in society who do not live long enough to see this great moderation are not spelt out by McCloskey. From the very different Marxist perspective, the reliance on the state to overturn Piketty's observation of rate of return to savings being higher than the rate of growth of GDP, $r > g$, is the central challenge. Roberts (2016, pp. 251–254) locates Piketty's $r > g$ relationship in the late twentieth century on a deeper understanding of Marx's long-run 'tendency of the rate of profit to fall' rather than Piketty's observation on the rise of neo-liberalism. The conclusion of this is that Piketty is identifying a symptom rather than a cause of inequality and therefore the solutions proposed by Piketty would also be insufficient to resolve the still deeper fundamental flaw in capitalist development. In addition, Tengely-Evans (2014) points to Piketty's intellectual linkage to neo-classical economic thinking with a continued reliance upon economic 'shocks' as the original explanation for the period when $g > r$ before the later reversing of this relationship. Specifically, the two World Wars and the later rise of neo-liberalism act as independent exogenous influences, unexplained ad-hoc expediencies, as primary weaknesses in Piketty's approach.

An alternative challenge to Piketty's understanding of inequality has also arisen from a focus of attention on global inequality rather than that across the advanced capitalist economies. Milanovic (2018) identified the emergence of an 'elephant curve' depicting inequality globally spanning an era of two decades from 1988. As shown in Chapter 1, viewed from a global scale, four distinct patterns of inequality are evident which collectively can be represented as an 'elephant curve'. First, at the elephant's tail, little change can be discerned for those at the bottom three deciles of the global income distribution. Subsistence farming and rural poverty continued to ensure that a significant level of the global population remained in absolute poverty untouched by globalisation of the late twentieth century. Indeed, the United Nation's Human Development Report (2016, p. 26) suggests that some 11% of the world's population lives in extreme poverty of less than $2 per day. The second element, contributing from the back to the head of the elephant curve, perhaps the most significant element saw the rapid development of global manufacturing bringing large numbers of rural workers and peasant farmers into wage labour market-based employment. Large-scale mass production urban factory systems saw rising real incomes for large proportions of the populations in developing economies, China and more latterly India were the key examples of this industrialisation. Incomes for those in the fourth through to the sixth and seventh income deciles rose rapidly as a proportion of the global income distribution. This, Milanovic suggests, is the origins of a new global middle class benefiting from rapid globalisation and developing the potential for new higher levels of demand for consumption goods. Thus, private consumption rose more rapidly than the supply of state provision of public goods leading, for example to mobile phone use and satellite TV use being evident in communities in which clean water and sanitation were yet to arrive.

The third element, the downward section of the elephant's trunk, can be understood to be the stagnant or falling real incomes for those in the developed world whose populations were the losers in this emergent globalisation era. Those who were previously in the eighth and ninth income deciles saw real falls in terms of global income shares. The process of de-industrialisation, increasing flexible labour markets weakening the redistributive effects of trade unions and movements from manufacturing into services led to stagnating, even falling real wages in large parts of the developed world. In the United States, as an example, average real wages declined continuously for three decades from the 1970s (Harvey, 2010, p. 13 and p. 62). Finally, the end of the elephant's trunk pointing upward was represented by the top 5% of the income distribution. This group, and even more so the top 1%, represented a new global elite that has gained 40% increases in income in the final two decades of the twentieth century. This elite was now global in composition with even those original members in the advanced economies struggling to maintain a foothold within this group. The top 12% of those in the United States can be found in this global top 1% while only the top 5% of the British income distribution have sufficient income to be included in this patrimonial elite. Globally the top 1% were found to account for almost 29% of all income and almost 46% of all asset wealth (Wolf, 2016).

Milanovic's analysis has been the subject to challenge from Piketty and co-authors, especially with reference to the extent to which a rise of a new middle-class can be identified. Milanovic's analysis may overstate the Kuznets-style equalisation in lower-income deciles when examined within a longer time framework according to Facundo, Chancel, Piketty, Saez and Zucman (2017 and 2018). However, while a debate exists over the development of a global middle-class within the income distribution at the highest level of the income distribution Milanovic's analysis is highly consistent with that of Piketty. The top 10% of the income distribution and the top 1% of the income distribution, even more so, has seen rapid increases in income and wealth over the last decades of the twentieth century compared to that of the other nine income deciles.

In the analysis within this chapter, we now wish to see if we can discern results consistent with those of Piketty or Milanovic by using the UKHLS, Understanding Society dataset.

Income data for the highest incomes

One of the central differences in the Milanovic data in contrast to that of the work of Piketty is the origins of their income data. There is no single accepted methodology of assessing wealth and high incomes in the literature (Atkinson, Piketty and Saez, 2011). Milanovic's results derive from cross-country household panel survey data whereas Piketty's primary dataset is derived from tax records and income shares, themselves derived from national income and expenditure accounts. Both methodologies face disadvantages. Household panel surveys disadvantages relate to the measurement of high income and wealth due to their utilisation of income bands rather than discrete income levels. Individuals in the highest income band are simply aggregated together if their income is above a pre-defined threshold. In the case of the use of income tax records and income shares estimations are required for the changing coverage of income tax in a population, missing data and tax avoidance (Atkinson, 1980, pp. 210–213).

In the case of the UKHLS Understanding Society dataset, the two most significant limitations lie in attempts to counteract an unwillingness of answer in questionnaire design. The use of an income band of £100,000 per annum for the highest earning individuals provides a solution to misreporting of earned income but a potential for misreporting of income remains in the reporting of non-labour income, such as return on investments data. Earned income above £100K is simply reported as the maximum, while non-earned income is reported at its actual level. Unearned income may be less reliable due to under reporting by participants in the UKHLS or inadvertent error due to the irregularity of its receipt.

A final difference with our analysis is again that throughout we focus upon a household's equivalised income after housing costs rather than individual's non-equivalised before housing cost income. As a result, we should not expect the results from the UKHLS data to provide us with definitive comparable results to the levels of income wealth and inequality in Piketty's nor Milanovic's approach. Rather, instead, we should focus on the trends and broad comparisons with other parts of the income distribution. The rest of this chapter now examines the UKHLS data for the highest household incomes to examine the extent to which we can identify the existence of a distinct social grouping for the highest-income households.

Wealthy households in the UKHLS

In Chapter 3, we examined extreme poverty by starting with an examination of household characteristics for those households located in the bottom income decile. While disadvantage through ill-health and disability or economic shocks through unemployment do not provide similar characteristics for explanations as to why a household might have the highest incomes and be located in the highest, or 10th, income decile, there are nevertheless other characteristics that can be identified as correlating with high income. High-income households will have access to income from both labour and non-labour income streams. Thus, we are interested in total household income and households are ranked in order of total income. As with Chapter 3, we follow a consistent methodological approach to the construction of our income variable, equivalised real monthly household income after housing costs, and to the household's mobility into and out of the highest income decile. In addition to that of Chapter 3, we also seek to determine if there is evidence that there is differentiation within the wealthiest 1% compared to the other 9% of the top income decile.

Again, as in our previous chapter, we start with wave B of the UKHLS dataset. **Table 4.1** highlights the numbers and percentages of households in the highest 10% of the income distribution, the 10th income decile. In the first column, we identify potential typologies of households leading to above-average household income. Columns 2–5 then provide comparative total numbers and percentages of the income distribution: in column 2 for the first nine income deciles, column 3 and 4 the highest (10th) income decile subdivided by the 90th–98th percentiles and the very highest 99th percentile. Finally, column 5, the total sample for the UKHLS.

It can be observed from **Table 4.1** that there are marked differences between households found to be in the highest income decile in comparison with the other nine income deciles. In addition, for those within the highest income decile, we can observe further differentiation. The highest 1% of the income distribution appear to hold characteristics important for determining the difference

TABLE 4.1 UKHLS Household Characteristics for the Highest Income Decile, Wave B (2011)

*Characteristic for Household Being in the 10th Decile**		*Household Income Decile*			
			10th Decile		
Total and Percentage		*1–9th Decile*	*90th–98th Percentiles (9%)*	*99th Percentile (1%)*	*UKHLS Total*
Wealth rich, income rich	Number	905	119	22	1046
	%	3.8%	5.1%	7.3%	4.0%
Business owner/ Partner	Number	767	189	71	1027
	%	3.2%	8.1%	23.5%	3.9%
Multiple Managerial & Professional jobs	Number	794	395	39	1228
	%	3.4%	17.0%	12.9%	4.7%
Single Managerial & Professional job	Number	3681	743	76	4500
	%	15.6%	31.9%	25.2%	17.1%
Single Migrant	Number	1845	124	13	1982
	%	7.8%	5.3%	4.3%	7.5%
Multiple Migrant	Number	3096	338	37	3471
	%	13.1%	14.5%	12.3%	13.2%
Multiple private sector employment	Number	812	23	2	837
	%	3.4%	1.0%	0.7%	3.2%
Single private sector employment	Number	3041	141	11	3193
	%	12.8%	6.1%	3.6%	12.1%
Multiple public sector employment	Count	138	10	0	148
	%	0.6%	0.4%	0.0%	0.6%
Single public sector employment	Number	1178	69	3	1250
	%	5.0%	3.0%	1.0%	4.8%
Multiple university education	Number	119	17	0	136
	%	0.5%	0.7%	0.0%	0.5%
Single university education	Number	978	48	8	1034
	%	4.1%	2.1%	2.6%	3.9%
Unexplained	Number	6315	112	20	6447
	%	26.7%	4.8%	6.6%	24.5%
Total	Number	23669	2328	302	26299
	%	100.0%	100.0%	100.0%	100.0%

Source: UK Household Longitudinal Study, Wave B (2011).

* The characteristics are in many cases mutually reinforcing and, therefore, the ordering in which they are chosen determines their significance.

between the highest one percentile and the other nine percentiles in the highest income decile.

In our first example, we have households having both high income from existing wealth through rent and dividend income combined with high income through employment, 'Wealth rich/Income rich'. This group has much greater prevalence in the highest income decile than the rest of the income distribution. Thus, for the first nine income deciles, 3.8% of the sample can be identified as 'Wealth rich/income rich' while the comparative figure for households within the 90th–98th income percentiles is 5.1% and even more starkly in the 99th income percentile the figure is almost double at 7.3%.

In our second household characteristic 'Business Owner/Partner,' this effect is even more strongly evident. Being a business owner or partner in a private sector company is a characteristic of just 3.2% of households in the first nine income deciles but accounts for 8.1% of households within the 90th–98th income percentile and 23.5% for the highest income percentile. The third characteristic within **Table 4.1** identified as more prevalent within the highest income decile is that of households with high-income employment, either as a single or a multiple-income household. High income from employment is defined as 'Managerial, Professional or Technical' employment under the standard classification methodology. In contrast to being 'Wealth rich/income rich' or a 'Business owner/Partner' however, high earned income shows a slightly different picture within the highest income decile itself. Single high-income households and multiple high-income households account for 3.4% and 15.6% of households respectively within the bottom nine income deciles. In the highest income decile, while still retaining its propensity of greater importance for those in the top income decile compared with the rest of the income distribution, it plays more of a significant role for those in the 90th–98th percentiles (17.0% and 31.9% respectively) than is the case for the top 1% (12.9% and 25.2% respectively).

Other characteristics such as ethnicity, educational attainment and public sector employment show either little difference (Migrant or Higher Education status) or is more prevalent within the rest of the income distribution than the highest income distribution (Public Sector employment). A final feature of interest worthy of considering is the extent to which the proportion of the income deciles are not accounted for by the characteristics chosen in **Table 4.1**. Whereas 26.7% of households in income deciles, one to nine do not fall into any of the categories listed the figure for the 90th–98th percentiles are only 4.8% and for the highest income percentile 6.0%.

We should note here one difference with the equivalent table in Chapter 3 in that in this case, our totals do add to 100% with each category being exclusive. In Chapter 3, we chose non-exclusive categories as many forms of disadvantage reinforce one another and can be considered to be intersecting whereas advantage is primarily exclusive with intersectionality playing little additional role. Despite this difference in approach, similar conclusions about these correlations can be drawn. There is evidence of a structural relationship between a household characteristics and high total household income within both the 90th–98th percentiles and the 99th percentile groups.

The significance of the correlations highlighted in **Table 4.1** can also be tested by the use of multinomial logit regression analysis (see Table 4.2) to ask the question which of these characteristics plays a statistically significant role in explaining a household being within the bottom nine income deciles compared to the highest income decile (and itself subdivided between the 90th–98th income percentiles and the highest 99th income percentile).

The first set of rows provided in **Table 4.2** show results for households in the top 90th–98th income percentiles compared to the other nine income deciles. Row 3 shows that a household containing at least one Wealth rich/Income rich individuals are positively correlated with a correlation coefficient of 0.26977 and that this correlation is statistically significant at the 5% level compared to the households in the bottom nine income deciles with a t-statistic = 2.41.[1] Rows seven to ten show that having at least one individual in the household with high-income employment (Managerial and Professional Job) or at least one member of the household with higher education are similarly all positively correlated and significant at the 5% level compared to households in the bottom nine income deciles.

TABLE 4.2 Multinomial Logistic Regression on Characteristics of UKHLS Households in the Highest Income Decile, Wave B (2011)

Households in Bottom Nine Income Deciles Compared to the 90th–98th Income Percentiles					
Variable	*Coefficient.*	*Std. Err.*	*t-stat*		
Wealth Rich and Income Rich	.2697717	.1118731	2.41		
Business Owner/Partner	.0492669	.0876993	0.56		
Single Migrant	−.17169	.0756952	−2.27		
Multiple Migrant	−.7304807	.1084477	−6.74		
Single Managerial and Professional Job	1.573191	.055991	28.10		
Multiple Managerial and Professional Jobs	2.361127	.0696534	33.90		
Single Higher Education	.5486354	.0537409	10.21		
Multiple Higher Education	.6997413	.0682553	10.25		
Constant	−3.483893	.0452588	−76.98		
Households in Bottom Nine Income Deciles Compared to the 99th Income Percentile					
Variable	*Coefficient.*	*Std. Err.*	*t-stat*		
Wealth Rich and Income Rich	.6549885	.2262	2.90		
Business Owner/Partner	1.590645	.1411593	11.27		
Single Migrant	−.1438543	.186847	−0.77		
Multiple Migrant	−1.477516	.3907668	−3.78		
Single Managerial and Professional Job	1.167229	.1456586	8.01		
Multiple Managerial and Professional Jobs	1.669963	.181653	9.19	Number of obs	27155
Single Higher Education	.7773625	.1371959	5.67	Pseudo R2	0.1406
Multiple Higher Education	.9184359	.1736912	5.29		
Constant	−5.535605	.1187122	−46.63		

Source: UK Household Longitudinal Study, Wave B (2011).

In contrast, however, households containing an individual with a migrant background are both negatively (correlation coefficients of −0.17169 for multiple migrant households and −0.73048 for single migrant households) and this negative correlation is statistically significant (t-statistic −2.27 and −6.74 respectively) compared to households in the bottom nine income deciles.

Finally, being a Business Owner/Partner while positively correlated with being in the 90th–98th income percentile with a positive correlation coefficient (0.0492669) it does not have a statistically significant relationship with a t-statistic (0.56).

The conclusion drawn from these statistically significant relationships is that the correlations are not random and the household characteristic holds a causative impact on the household's position within the income distribution.

In the second half of **Table 4.2**, we can view the same household relationships replicated, but in this case, comparing the position of the highest income percentile (the 99th income percentile) with the nine deciles below it. In doing so, we can ascertain the extent to which stratification within the highest income decile prevails.

The results in the second half of **Table 4.2** show that while many of the relationships found in first part of the table still hold, with their coefficients retaining the same positive or negative sign as the first regression, their t-statistics indicating the degree of significance has fallen. Thus, for households containing at least one individual in a Managerial or Professional job their correlation coefficient is still positive (coefficient 1.1672 for Single Managerial job and 1.6699 for Multiple Managerial jobs in a household) but their measure of significance, while still significant at the 5% level, has fallen from 28.10 to 8.01 and 33.90 to 9.19 for Single and Multiple households respectively. This implies that the extent of differentiation between the characteristics of the bottom nine deciles and the very highest 1% of the income distribution has fallen for the four examples of single and multiple managerial and professional jobs and for households with one or more individuals with experience of higher education.

In contrast, however, being a Business Owner/Partner is now of much higher significance for being within the highest 1% of the income distribution. Having a 'Business Owner/Partner' in the household is both positively correlated (coefficient 0. 1.5906) and has the highest t-statistic value 11.27 of all the results for households being in the highest income percentile compared to the lowest nine income deciles. It can also be observed that the correlation coefficients for being wealth rich and income rich or being a business owner are larger than in the initial regression results in the top half of **Table 4.2**. So, while being wealth rich and income rich had a positive correlation coefficient initially of 0.26977, this had increased to 0.65488 in importance in influencing a household's location within the 99th income percentile. For business owners, this rise was still greater with an almost four-fold increase in the correlation coefficient from 0.4926 for the 90th–98th percentiles to 1.5906 for the 99th percentile of households relative to the bottom nine income deciles.

The results for the 1% in **Table 4.2** reinforce our evidence that the composition of the highest income percentile is indeed different to both the rest of the highest income decile and that of the other nine income deciles and that these differences have a structural component linked to the household characteristics.

While the evidence for **Table 4.2** demonstrates differences within the highest income decile, with households that include business owners/partners and those with both high wealth and income being overly represented within top 1% there is also a need to understand the longevity of this association. The logit regression analysis reported in **Table 4.2** highlights that the UKHLS data is consistent with Piketty's analysis of segmentation within the richest households. However, Piketty goes further to explain this causation as arising from returns to assets exceeding returns to labour as a permanent feature of inequality emerging in the last quarter of the twentieth century. Thus, a further examination of the UKHLS for the highest household income decile is, therefore, to look at the extent to which there is mobility in and out of the income decile. Specifically, we wish to examine the extent to which a household's location in the 90th–98th or 99th percentile is a relatively permanent effect. Again, replicating the approach in Chapter 3, we start with wave B of the UKHLS dataset. **Table 4.3** shows the level of attrition from the highest income decile through to wave G of the dataset.

Comparing columns 2 and 3 of **Table 4.3**, allows us to follow households through the period of the UKHLS from wave B to wave G. We observe that in most waves the proportion of households exiting the top 99th percentile is lower than for the 90th–98th percentiles. Within one year moving from Wave B to Wave C shows that 37.9% of households in the 90th–98th percentiles moved out of this group compared to 31.8% of the highest 99th percentile. In the final column of **Table 4.3**, highlighting the total across all waves B to G of the UKHLS we

TABLE 4.3 Household Attrition from the UKHLS Highest Income Decile, Waves B–G (2011–2016)

		Highest Income Decile		
Household Exiting the Highest Income Decile Each Wave		*90th–98th Percentile*	*99th Percentile*	*Total*
Total in wave B	Number	1276	154	1430
	%	100.0%	100.0%	100.0%
As early as Wave C	Number	483	49	532
	%	37.9%	31.8%	37.2%
Only by Wave D	Number	214	19	233
	%	16.8%	12.3%	16.3%
Only by Wave E	Number	141	12	153
	%	11.1%	7.8%	10.7%
Only by Wave F	Number	75	13	88
	%	5.9%	8.4%	6.2%
Only by Wave G	Number	55	6	61
	%	4.3%	3.9%	4.3%
Remaining in top 10% throughout	Number	308	55	363
	%	24.1%	35.7%	25.4%

Source: UK Household Longitudinal Study, Waves B–G (2011–2016).

observe that 25.4% of households in the highest income decile retain their position relative to the whole income distribution over the period. However, households in the 99th percentile of the income distribution are around 50% more likely to retain their position in the income distribution than the rest of those households in the highest income decile. Thus, while 24.1% of households in the 90th–98th percentiles remain in the highest income decile this figure reaches 35.7% for the wealthiest 99th percentile in the income distribution. A household's position within the top 99th percentile of the income distribution appears to be a feature of the origins of their household income and this is a more permanent feature than households elsewhere in the highest income decile, again consistent with Piketty's assumption of a permanent shift in the income distribution of the population.

A final examination of the effect of wealth comes from the national and regional distribution of those in the highest income decile within the UK. **Table 4.4** examines where in the UK the top income decile households are located.

TABLE 4.4 Population Weighted Distribution of UKHLS Households in Top Income Decile, Wave B (2011)

				10th Decile		
Region Total and Percentage within the Region			*1st–9th Decile*	*90th–98th Percentile (9%)*	*99th Percentile (1%)*	*Total*
	London	Number	3491	457	71	4019
		%	86.9%	11.4%	1.8%	100.0%
	South East	Number	2749	391	60	3200
		%	85.9%	12.2%	1.9%	100.0%
	South West	Number	1856	165	16	2037
		%	91.1%	8.1%	0.8%	100.0%
	East Midlands	Number	1763	140	15	1918
		%	91.9%	7.3%	0.8%	100.0%
	West Midlands	Number	2113	180	17	2310
		%	91.5%	7.8%	0.7%	100.0%
	East of England	Number	2050	240	28	2318
		%	88.4%	10.4%	1.2%	100.0%
	North East	Number	1068	55	7	1130
		%	94.5%	4.9%	0.6%	100.0%
	North West	Number	2635	231	25	2891
		%	91.1%	8.0%	0.9%	100.0%
	York and Humber	Number	2033	131	17	2181
		%	93.2%	6.0%	0.8%	100.0%
	Scotland	Number	1706	178	29	1913
		%	89.2%	9.3%	1.5%	100.0%
	northern Ireland	Number	1054	67	10	1131
		%	93.2%	5.9%	0.9%	100.0%
	Wales	Number	1151	93	7	1251
		%	92.0%	7.4%	0.6%	100.0%
Total		Number	23669	2328	302	26299
		%	90.0%	8.9%	1.1%	100.0%

Source: UK Household Longitudinal Study, Wave B (2011).

Table 4.4 examines the constituent nations and regions of the UK by population share to determine the extent to which the highest incomes are located.[2] **Table 4.4** shows that there is not a highly concentrated geographical distribution of high-income households in the UK, although some concentrations can be identified. A concentration of households within the highest income decile can be found in London (11.4%) and the South East (12.2%) for the 90th–98th percentiles and London (1.8%), the South East (1.9%) and Scotland (1.5%) for the 99th percentile. In contrast, those areas of the UK with the highest proportion of households in the bottom nine income deciles include the North East of England (94.5%), northern Ireland (93.2%) and Yorkshire and Humberside (93.2%)

Conclusion

The recent revival in an interest in inequality within the academic literature has shifted attention away from solely examining the extent to which poverty exists to an examination of the whole of the income distribution. Hitherto, debates over the levels of inequality had focused predominantly on the distribution of incomes lower down the income distribution. In order to examine questions of inequality rather than poverty, an examination of the characteristics and extent of income and wealth disparities among those within the top of the income distribution has been a feature of this academic scholarship. Most notably this has focused upon data developed by the work of both Piketty (2014) and Milanovic (2018). This scholarship has also drawn attention to the rise of an elite whose incomes have grown significantly faster than the rest of the population. The highest income decile, and within this the highest income percentile, have seen rapid growth in their incomes over the past three decades and this has been associated with an increasing concentration of not simply income but asset wealth. In this chapter, we sought to examine the extent to which this understanding can be identified within the UKHLS dataset.

This chapter, therefore, examined the extent to which the highest income decile, and specifically the highest income percentile, can be understood to have specific characteristics relative to the rest of the income distribution. In doing so, the chapter acted to test some of the concepts included within the inequality literature. The findings of the chapter demonstrate there is consistent evidence within the UKHLS for the conclusions found within the wider inequality literature. Namely, households in the top income decile and even more so the top 1% of the income distribution have specific characteristics that differentiate them from the rest of the sample population. Further, the characteristics of the top 1% also provide a longevity to their position within the income distribution which limits mobility within the highest income decile.

Data from the UKHLS demonstrates that we can indeed discern specific characteristics of the wealthiest in the population. They are found to be beneficiaries of asset wealth and from income derived from ownership of businesses and partnerships.

Together with the evidence provided in Chapter 3, we can suggest the income distribution at both extremes is highly socially structured and not derived from a random set of household characteristics. A household's position within the lowest and highest deciles of the income distribution is strongly associated with their household characteristics and these characteristics lead households to be more fixed within the income distribution the more they are located towards the extreme ends of the income distribution. Not only is extreme poverty a socially structural feature of contemporary society but so too is extreme wealth.

In the next section of this volume, we turn to the question of what forms public policy might take which seeks to address these levels of inequality within the UK through redistribution of resources. Any redistribution of resources from the higher end of the income distribution to the lower end will increase equality. Therefore, we should not simply be interested in the extent to which re-distribution may be effective but also the extent to which it can be operationalised within a welfare and labour market system in which inequalities have structural roots.

Notes

1 For readers unfamiliar with regression analysis, for a variable to be positively correlated with another their coefficient must have a positive sign, as in column 2 of **Table 4.2** and to be statistically significant at the 5% level a t-stat greater or equal to 1.94 is required in column 4. The higher the t-statistic the more statistically significant a variable is considered to be. See Chapter 2, for more detail.

2 In order to avoid the bias that a region with twice the population of a less populated region would superficially seem to have a higher concentration of wealthy households if it had twice the number of wealthy adults, we need to use a measure based on population shares.

References

Alcroft, D.H. (1993), *The European Economy 1914–1990* (3rd edition), London: Routledge.

Angus, I. (2016), *Facing the Anthropocene: Fossil Capitalism and the Crisis of the Earth System*, New York: Monthly Review Press.

Atkinson, A. (ed.) (1980), *Wealth, Income and Inequality* (2nd edition), Oxford: Oxford University Press, pp. 210–213.

Atkinson, A.B., Piketty, T. and Saez, E. (2011), Top Incomes in the Long Run of History. *Journal of Economic Literature* 49(1), pp. 3–71.

Beveridge, W. (1967), *Full Employment in a Free Society: A Report by Lord Beveridge*, London: George Allen & Unwin.

Burke-Leacock, E. (2008), *Myths of Male Dominance: Collected Articles on Women Cross-Culturally*, Illinois: Haymarket.

Callinicos, A.T. (2000), *Equality*, Cambridge: Polity Press.

Casson, M. (2003), *The Entrepreneur: An Economic Theory*, Cheltenham, Hampshire: Edward Elgar Publishing.

Childe, G.V. (1965), *What Happened in History*, London: Penguin.

Cook, S. (1974), Structural Substantivism: A Critical Review of Marshall Shalins' Stone Age Economics'. *Comparative Studies in Society and History* 16(3), pp. 355–379.

De Ste Croix, G.E.M. (1981), *The Class Struggle in the Ancient Greek World: From the Archaic Age to the Arab Conquests*, Bodmin, Cornwall: Duckworth Press.

Elliott, L. and Atkinson, D. (2016), *Europe Isn't Working*, New Haven:Yale University Press.

Facundo, A., Chancel, L., Piketty, T., Saez, E. and Zucman, G. (2017), The Elephant Curve of Global Inequality and Growth, *WID. World Working Papers Series* 2017/20.

Facundo, A., Chancel, L., Piketty, T., Saez, E. and Zucman, G. (2018), *The World Inequality Report 2018*, Cambridge: Harvard University Press, available at http://wir2018.wid.world/ accessed 20th May 2018.

Flannery, K. and Marcus, J. (2012), *The Creation of Inequality: How Our Prehistoric Ancestors Set the Stage for Monarchy, Slavery and Empire*, Cambridge, MA: Harvard University Press.

Golson, J. and Gardner, D.S. (1990), Agriculture and Sociopolitical Organization in New Guinea Highlands Prehistory. *Annual Review of Anthropology* 9, pp. 395–417.

Harman, C. (1999), *A People's History of the World*, London: Bookmarks.

Harvey, D. (2010), *The Enigma of Capital: And the Crisis of Capitalism*, London: Exmouth Books.

Kirkch, P.V. (1991), Prehistoric Exchange in Western Melanesia, *Annual Review of Anthropology* 20, pp. 141–165.

Krugman, P. (1994), *Peddling Prosperity: Economic Sense and Nonsense in the Age of Diminished Expectations*, New York: W.W. Norton & Co., pp. 245–280.

Kuznets, S. (1955), Economic Growth and Income Inequality. *American Economic Review* 45(March), pp. 1–28.

Marx, K. (1970), *Capital: A Critique of Political Economy*, Vol. 1, London: Lawrence & Wishart.

Marx, K. (1980), Wages, Prices and Profit, in K. Marx and F. Engels, *Selected Writings in One Volume*, London: Lawrence and Wishart.

Marx, K. and Engels, F. (1980), *Selected Writings in One Volume*, London: Lawrence and Wishart.

Massucato, M. (2018), *The Entrepreneurial State: Debunking Public vs. Private Sector Myths*, London: Penguin.

McCloskey, D.N. (2017), Measured, Unmeasured, Mismeasured, and Unjustified Pessimism: A Review Essay of Thomas Piketty's Capital in the Twenty-First Century, *Erasmus Journal of Philosophy and Economics*, available at http://www.deirdremccloskey.org/docs/pdf/PikettyReviewEssay.pdf accessed 3rd February 2018.

Meagher, M. (2020), Competition *Is Killing US: How Business Is Harming Our Society and Planet – and What We Do About It*, London: Penguin.

Milanovic, B. (2018), *Global Inequality: A New Approach for the Age of Globalization*, Cambridge, MA: Harvard University Press.

Milward, A.S. (1992), *The European Rescue of the Nation-State*, London: Routledge.

North, D.C., (1991), Institutions, Journal of Economic Perspectives, 5(1), pp. 97–112.

Olson, M. (1971), *The Logic of Collective Action: Public Goods and the Theory of Groups*, Cambridge, MA: Harvard University Press.

Olson, M. (1982), *The Rise and Decline of Nations: Economic Growth, Stagflation, and Social Rigidities*, New Haven: Yale University Press.

Piketty, T. (2014), *Capital in the Twenty-First Century*, Cambridge, MA: Harvard University Press.

Rawls, J. (1985), Justice as Fairness: Political Not Metaphysical. *Philosophy and Public Affairs* 14(Summer), pp. 223–251.

Raworth, K. (2017), *Doughnut Economics: Seven Ways to Think Like a 21st Century Economist*, London: Random House.

Roberts, M. (2016), *The Long Depression: How It Happened, Why It Happened and What Happens Next*, Chicago, IL: Haymarket Books.

Roll, E. (1953), *The History of Economic Thought*, London: Faber & Faber.

Schumpter, J. (1994), *Capitalism, Socialism and Democracy*, London: Routledge.
Sen, A. (1995), *Inequality Re-Examined*, Cambridge, MA: Harvard University Press.
Shaikh, A. (2016), *Capitalism: Competition, Conflict, Crisis*, Oxford: Oxford University Press.
Shalin, M.D. (1988), *Stone-Age Economics*, London: Routledge.
Tengely-Evans, T. (2014), Piketty and Marx. *International Socialism Journal*, 143, pp. 177–186.
United Nation. (2016), *Human Development Report 2016: Human Development for Everyone*, New York: United Nations Development Programme.
Varoufakis, Y. (2016), *And the Weak Suffer What They Must? Europe's Crisis and America's Economic Future*, London: The Bodley Head.
Wolf, M. (2016), Global income inequality is falling – but widening disparities within nations present huge challenges: A review of Branko Milanovic Global Inequality: A New Approach for the Age of Globalization, *Financial Times*, 14th April available at https://www.ft.com/content/13603aa2-0185-11e6-ac98-3c15a1aa2e62 accessed 3rd July 2018.

5

INEQUALITY AND DEVOLUTION

Localised solutions to poverty and inequality

Introduction

In the earlier chapters of this work, the focus of attention was on the examination of the structural nature of inequality and poverty within the UK. As highlighted in Chapter 2, the UK Household Longitudinal Study, Understanding Society (UKHLS) dataset permits both the full composition of households to be identified and, in addition, the ability to track those households over time to examine mobility. Utilising these features of the dataset Chapters 3 and 4, demonstrated those at the extreme ends of the income distribution showed low levels of mobility. Their extreme poverty and extreme wealth respectively were shown to be a long-run characteristic of the household. In addressing the extent to which these outcomes for households can be changed, the next chapters in this book examine potential policy avenues. Specifically, in this chapter, we examine the development of devolution and the de-centralisation of policy leavers while examining debates over universality and means-testing of re-distributional policies in Chapter 6.

Devolution is one of the mechanisms by which policy towards poverty and inequality has been enacted with the devolution of powers focusing particularly upon the areas provision most associated with the social wage, namely health and education This chapter, therefore, seeks to assess whether changes in the governance structure across the UK can be identified as impacting on income inequality in the UKHLS dataset.

Devolution in the UK has been one of the major institutional changes in the architecture of government in the twenty-first century. Keating describes this process as the creation of 'a complex, multilevel polity, through a process of asymmetrical devolution' enhancing and strengthening government's institutional infrastructure within a unified singular state (2007, p. 1). Alternatively, it can be

DOI: 10.4324/9781315179957-5

understood within a wider, international context, as the breaking apart of large national state formations in an era whereby the interconnectedness brought about by globalisation leaves little function for large state structures. As Stiglitz proposes, individual economies increasingly reflect the 'global governance without global government' (2002, p. 21) operating within the world economy. Thus, a diminution of state functions has occurred as global inter-relationships and coordination has grown.

Devolution within the UK developed from 1999, first in two constituent nations of the UK, namely Scotland and Wales, and the administration of six counties within northern Ireland. Shortly afterwards, it was followed by the establishment of the Greater London Authority in 2000. Devolution has since become an established and deeply rooted feature of the governmental institutional framework across the UK. From 2014, the devolution of central government powers was further extended to smaller regions within England, all be it in a more limited way than in the devolved administrations, with the introduction of elected regional mayors for Greater Manchester, and similarly, from 2016 in the Liverpool City Region, the Tees Valley, West of England and the West Midlands. Devolution within England was underpinned by legislation within the *Cities and Local Government Devolution Act (2016)* providing for regional mayors, not with legislative powers but instead with administrative functions, for the management of regional functions requiring coordination across local government boundaries. Simultaneously, the *Scotland Act* (2016) gave still greater devolved powers to the most far-reaching example of devolution within the UK, that of the Scottish Parliament. The Scotland Act facilitated the option to 'substitute' a Scottish income tax for the UK income tax (2016, section 13) and for the introduction of new welfare provision (2016, section 28). These new powers themselves derived from the UK Government's response to the demands for independence raised during the 2014 Independence referendum which saw a narrow majority for Scotland remaining within the UK.

Support for devolution, in general, has increased over time, within the most extensive case of Scotland 51% of the population now agreeing with the statement '*The Scottish Parliament should make all the decisions for Scotland*' (Scottish Centre for Social Science Research, 2015). Even within northern Ireland, where the Assembly has a more chequered history and was suspended for three years between 2017 and 2020, evidence from Social Attitudes Surveys implies devolution has increased its recognition within public perception. While the existence of the northern Ireland Assembly is bound up in debates over the unification of Ireland, support for the continuation of the Assembly has coincided with both a fall in support for northern Ireland remaining as part of the UK and simultaneously no increase in support for the unification of Ireland over time. As the British Social Attitudes Survey suggests:

> while commitment to the maintenance of the Union may have been eroded, there is no sign of increased support for reunification with the rest of Ireland.

> Between 1989 and 2006 support oscillated around an average of 23 per cent, without any discernible trend in either direction.
>
> *(2012, 30, figure 6.4, p.153)*

Such a contradictory result suggests a rise in support for a devolved form of government within northern Ireland coming from both the different perspectives supporting and opposing Irish reunification.

While the case of northern Ireland highlights distinct and indeed unique differences in debates over the role of devolution the widespread support for devolved government and administrations can be found throughout the regions and nations of the UK, where devolution has emerged. Despite differences in ideological starting points for devolution, the identification of the proximity to decision making, the advantages of local knowledge in the design and implantation of policy initiatives and the accountability of decision-makers to their constituents continued to act as a particularly important driver for increased devolved powers (Kay, 2003; Keating, 2003). A lack of 'voice' at the UK level continues to be identified as a rationale for alternative mechanisms for regional or national autonomy with the aim of encouraging policy divergence and innovative unique local solutions to economic disparities. Keating specifically appeals to notions of distinct cultural and political differences facilitating these changes and, in the Scottish case, a desire for a 'distinct Scottish model' of government provision (Keating, 2005).

The desire of developing divergent, locally focused, policy is most apparent in the areas associated with income inequalities between nations and regions. The effectiveness of decentralisation and devolution to address income inequality is, however, significantly limited by the extent to which fiscal powers have been devolved and devolved institutions themselves are prevented from ensuring direct financial control is under local decision making. Sacchi and Salotti (2014, p. 206) critically examine the impact of fiscal decentralisation and its impact on income inequality across Western Europe finding that the higher the level of fiscal decentralisation the greater the level of income inequality among households within a country. A pessimistically consistent picture emerges of fiscal decentralisation in which fiscal decentralisation is understood as facilitating both a reduction in inter-regional transfers from richer to poorer regions and, in addition, increasing the likelihood of competitive tax-cutting policies derived from neoliberal supply-side economic development policies in a 'race to the bottom' between regions (Kim, Hong and Ha, 2003; Rodríguez-Pose and Ezcurra, 2010; Tselios, Rodríguez-Pose, Pike, Tomaney and Torrisi, 2012). Together these two pressures are understood to ensure devolution operates to intensify neoliberal economic objectives rather than provide an institutional impediment to the transmission of neoliberal economic policy from a centralised state powers to local administrations. What is largely lacking from this literature, however, is the examination of the impact of devolution on intra-regional inequalities, income inequalities within the devolved nation or region. Morelli and Seaman provided one of the first examples of this work by exploring income inequalities within nations and regions. They concluded that there was little evidence of devolution impacting income inequalities within the devolved nations of Scotland and Wales (2007, pp. 523–538).

Familiarity with the existence of devolved parliaments and administrations may play an important part in explaining the growth of popular support for devolution policies, bolstering the justification for devolution in terms of appeals to localism and accountability for decision making in public bodies (Bromley, 2006). However, within this support is evident a broad range of spatially focused, yet contested, approaches to economic rationales for these developments (Pike, Andrés Rodríguez-Pose and Tomaney, 2007; Mooney and Scott, 2012; Keating, 2017).

From a neoliberal informed economic perspective, devolution provides a mechanism for the weakening and hollowing out of UK state-wide institutions where underfunding of state provision of welfare systems leads to the retreat of the state and the deepening of market provision for goods and services. Devolved administrations, third sector and private provision are, within this framework, suggested to be more efficient and responsive than a unified-state wide provision (Centre for Social Justice, 2006). Within the UK the *Health and Social Care Act* (2012) provides one example of the means by which decentralisation within the English National Health Service (NHS) was understood as a means to open state sectors to greater private provision. The abolition of centralised NHS Trusts in England and replacement of their functions with decentralised Clinical Commissioning Groups (CCGs) ensured the link between community care and acute hospital care no longer automatically existed. CCGs could, but were not obliged to, contract with local NHS hospital providers for care and instead could now contract with a wide range of alternative providers. However, as the health research unit the Kings Fund reported one negative impact of this new framework was that 'the benefits provided by the shift towards CCGs co-commissioning primary care could be compromised by potential conflicts of interest, reductions in running cost budgets and strained relationships with fellow GPs and NHS England' (Holder, Robertson, Ross, Bennett, Gosling and Curry, 2015, p. 5). The experience in England was in stark contrast to that of the devolved governments and administrations, where less reform of structures of health provision took place. Surprisingly perhaps, the resulting divergence in health policy then originated from the remnants of the centralised UK governance structures rather than from the devolved administrations and governments themselves.

Devolution from a Keynesian perspective provided a means to mobilise local state actors in a developmental framework enhancing, if not replacing, private market provision. Again in relation to the NHS devolved administrations in the countries of Wales and Scotland, the approach taken by the NHS has seen the retention of centralised funding control and direct relationships between acute and primary providers of health care (Wales Health and Social Care Department, 2005; McCafferty, 2006). In so doing, the scope for private provision has not expanded, as is the case in the English NHS. Within this perspective, devolution has been perceived as providing a bulwark against the deepening of market incentives into state provision of services.

Within Higher Education, a similar picture emerges of the devolved administrations and governments acting to limit the extent to which private market provision expanded, underpinned by student tuition fees occurring in the English system, via the limitation, or abolition in the case of Scotland, of student tuition fees. McGettigan (2013) located the role played by the creation of a market for higher education and a system of student loans facilitating the breaking apart and privatisation of a UK-wide unified Higher Education network of providers. Within this new environment, Holmwood, Hickey and Wallis (2016, pp. 9–12) emphasised the lack of sustainability created within this new market for higher education. Importantly, this introduction of the market into Higher Education did not reduce the unified state's role in funding of higher education, rather the reverse. Now long-term debt in the form of guaranteed government repayments for student loans replaced current expenditure on direct funding to universities in what McGettigan identifies as the financialisation of the sector (2013, pp. 172–184).

A deeper more historical critique of the perceived failures of the centralised UK-national state has also been made. The UK state's withdrawal from industrial policy in the 1980s and failure to support regional economic development led to demands for greater local autonomy and decision-making powers. This was particularly in nations and regions where deindustrialisation from the 1970s was at its most acute. One such early example of this was the publication in 1975 of the *Red Paper on Scotland*, edited by Gordon Brown who later became UK Prime Minster from 2007–2010, which set out a blueprint for an alternative economic strategy within a devolved Scotland. Central to the *Red Paper on Scotland* was an understanding of the structural limitations of economic development with a long-run relative decline of manufacturing and failure to develop a modernising state structure (Brown, 1975). Here, the devolved administrations are understood as providing opportunities for more responsive and interventionist industrial policy in contrast to that of the UK-level government. While in its infancy, examples of the potential for industrial policy can be recognised with the Scottish Government's nationalisation of key infrastructure facilities including Prestwick airport in 2013 and the return to public ownership of rail services as the franchise with the private provider ends in 2022 (Scottish Government, 2017; BBC, 2021). Similar returns to public ownership of rail services were also announced in Wales from 2021 (BBC, 2020).

Still more recently, the revival of regional development policy has emerged through the reappearance of concepts such as the 'Northern Powerhouse'. Emanating within the northern English, devolved administrations the Northern Powerhouse Partnership seeks to co-ordinate planning, transport and infrastructure investment within a model of regional development. As the first report of the Northern Powerhouse Partnership emphasised, 'The rationale for the Northern Powerhouse is driven by the economic concept of agglomeration, which essentially means economies of scale' (2017, p. 17).

This understanding of regional and national development utilises models of devolution embedded within an economic framework of comparative advantage in which barriers to trade and institutional restrictions upon specialisation reduce economic welfare delivered through trade flows (Stigler, 1957; Sloman, 1997). Within the framework of comparative advantage, the movement of goods, services and factors of production are free to move across geographies such that prices provide an accurate reflection of the opportunity cost of production. Thus, reducing transportation costs within regions and devolved nations provides additional comparative advantages for firms within private markets as supply-side reforms reduce transaction costs. Yet, in reality, markets do not correspond to these neo-classical models of homogenous factors of production. Trade may be able to flow freely within a unified state structure but the economic actors and the institutions determining these flows themselves have market power and are capable of determining factor prices through their dominant market positions. Thus, de-industrialisation through the 1980s and 1990s failed to lead to a revival of new industries as factor prices fell in regions with newly created excess supplies of land and labour. In contrast, de-industrialisation led to widening disparities with still greater concentrations of economic wealth in the already richer geographies of the unified UK economy. The result of these processes was that unified states further encouraged concentrations of wealth and exacerbated regional disparities rather than ensured redistributive outcomes.

The opposite outcomes of comparative advantage models led to a reassessment of models of comparative advantage among more Keynesian-based approaches within economics. The work of Krugman (1994, pp. 130–150), Stiglitz (2002) and Varoufakis (2015), for example, identified the dominant position played by key economic centres of wealth as the cause of these continuing disparities. Within their Keynesian focused framework industrial policy and state support, in the form of regional policy and devolution of decision-making powers, seeks to provide the policy initiatives and institutions aimed at addressing unequal development within the devolved areas arising from free market-based comparative advantage outcomes created in unified states.

As can be seen, regional development within a devolution context readily spans both neo-classical supply-side economics and Keynesian macro-economic approaches and can be presented in a de-politicised technocratic managerialism of local development within a fixed budgetary framework.

In summary, devolution is understood as a mechanism to provide services in a de-centralised form with the aim of providing demonstrably superior outcomes to local populations. This may take the form of economic development and growth or alternatively in terms of levels and quality of service provision for local populations from a pre-determined budget set by central government. Support for fiscal decentralisation and the devolving of greater political and economic decision making can be understood then as rooted within the market failure of the 'free-trade' model dominating within unified states in an era of globalisation. It is thus economic inequalities that have ensured calls for devolution of centralised powers have arisen and demands for greater devolution of budgetary, as well as expenditure powers, have evolved once devolved administrations became established and legitimised by their constituent populations. Within the UK, it is only in Scotland where devolution has extended to facilitating additional forms of taxation and welfare provision to date. Yet, the conclusions arising from studies of devolution and inequality suggest much greater government intent is required to enforce redistributive outcomes through the introduction of redistributive policies if devolution is to address poverty and income inequality (Morelli and Seaman, 2007; Rodríguez-Pose, Ezcurra, 2010; Tselios, Rodríguez-Pose, Pike, Tomaney and Torrisi, 2012).

In the rest of this chapter, we seek to establish whether we can find evidence from the UKLHS Understanding Society dataset of the impact of devolution on income inequality.

Income inequality

As with all other analyses in this book, we are interested in the extent to which equivalised real monthly household income after housing costs (eNMHI) shows variation across the different regions and nations in the UK. In order to examine this question, it is necessary to aggregate data into larger regions and nations within the UK to provide sufficiently large sample sizes to permit this analysis. **Table 5.1** highlights the difference in monthly household income between the poorest nations and regions of Wales and northern Ireland and the richest in the South of England and Scotland, using the Understanding Society dataset Waves A–G (2010–2016). While real household income (eNMHI), in 2010 prices, has risen in the richest area, namely the South of England from £2,585 to £3,179, from 2010–2016 they have stagnated from £2,175 to £2,174 in Wales. In order to represent these differences more readily, we can convert these absolute incomes into index numbers, using a three-year moving average, as shown in **Table 5.2** and displayed graphically in **Figure 5.1**. **Table 5.2** and **Figure 5.1** show that the relative position of the richest and poorest regions has remained static. Thus, the South of England's relative position, to the UK average, has increased marginally from an index number of 108.4 to 109.4, while in Wales the relative position has similarly changed marginally

TABLE 5.1 Regional and Devolved Nation Income Distribution £ (Equivalised Monthly Household Income Net of Housing Costs eNMHI), Wave A (2010) to Wave G (2016)

	Data Period						
Region	*Wave A*	*Wave B*	*Wave C*	*Wave D*	*Wave E*	*Wave F*	*Wave G*
South of England	2,585	2,802	2,903	2,985	3,041	3,101	3,179
English Midlands	2,336	2,532	2,629	2,715	2,719	2,779	2,807
North of England	2,224	2,430	2,502	2,565	2,612	2,632	2,688
Scotland	2,606	2,771	2,797	2,884	2,889	3,001	3,020
northern Ireland	2,166	2,210	2,298	2,365	2,489	2,447	2,499
Wales	2,175	2,368	2,435	2,558	2,493	2,617	2,714

Source: UKHLS Waves A–G (2010–2016).

TABLE 5.2 Regional and Devolved Nation Income Distribution Index (Equivalised Monthly Household Income Net of Housing Costs eNMHI), Wave A (2010) to Wave G (2016), three-year moving average (UK = 100)

	Data Period				
Region	*Waves A–C*	*Waves B–D*	*Waves C–E*	*Waves D–F*	*Waves E–G*
South of England	108.4	108.8	109.0	109.1	109.4
English Midlands	98.0	98.6	98.5	98.1	97.5
North of England	93.6	93.8	93.8	93.3	93.1
Scotland	107.0	105.8	104.7	104.8	104.6
northern Ireland	87.4	86.0	87.3	87.2	87.3
Wales	91.2	92.1	91.4	91.6	91.8

Source: UKHLS Waves A–G (2010–2016).

from 91.2 to 91.8. **Table 5.2** and **Figure 5.1** also highlight that dispersion of monthly average household income around the UK average of 100 is also consistent. The South of England and Scotland are consistently above the UK average, ranging from index numbers of 104.6 to 109.4, for the measure of equivalised real net monthly household income after housing costs (eNMHI) throughout the period, while northern Ireland and Wales are consistently below the UK average ranging between 87.2 and 92.1.

To what extent can these differences in income now be quantified in relation to inequality within nations and regions is what we now examine. **Table 5.3** and **Figure 5.2** complete the descriptive picture of the data. In **Table 5.3**, we can identify the South of England not only having the highest absolute and relative average household income but with a Gini coefficient measure of inequality ranging from 0.39424 to −0.37847, it has the highest level of income inequality in all years of the data. A Gini coefficient is a measure of inequality ranging

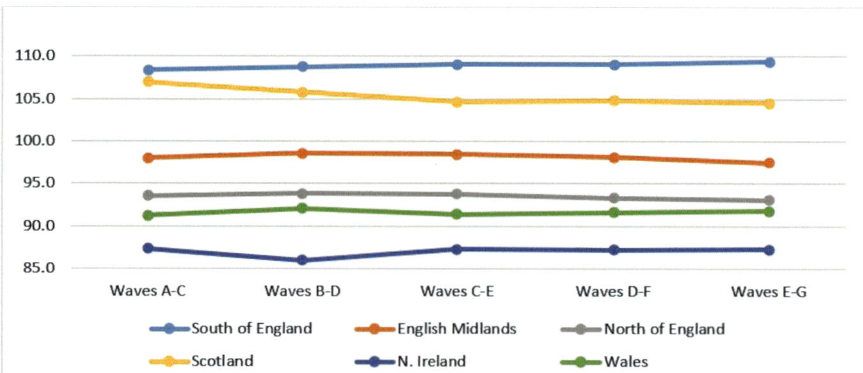

FIGURE 5.1 Regional and Devolved Nations Income Distribution Index (Equivalised Monthly Household Income Net of Housing Costs eNMHI), Wave A (2010) to Wave G (2016), three-year moving average (UK = 100)

TABLE 5.3 Regional and Devolved Nations Gini coefficients (Equivalised Real Monthly Household Income Net of Housing Costs eNMHI), Waves A–G (2010–2016)

	Data Period				
Region	*Waves A–C*	*Waves B–D*	*Waves C–E*	*Waves D–F*	*Waves E–G*
South of England	0.39424	0.38067	0.37764	0.38008	0.37847
English Midlands	0.37728	0.36031	0.35196	0.35316	0.35287
North of England	0.36166	0.34908	0.34519	0.34800	0.35165
Scotland	0.36007	0.34835	0.33929	0.34054	0.34058
northern Ireland	0.34129	0.32166	0.32106	0.31843	0.33409
Wales	0.34449	0.32830	0.32114	0.32395	0.32399

Source: UKHLS Waves A–G (2010–2016).

from 0 (perfect equality) to 1 (perfect inequality). Details of the Gini coefficient measurement can be found in Chapter 2. Similarly, northern Ireland, followed by Wales, consistently have the lowest levels of inequality *n* all years. In the case of northern Ireland, this ranges from a Gini coefficient of 0.32106 between Waves C and E rising to 0.34129 between Waves A and C.

Figure 5.2 however clearly also highlights another important relevant result. The measure of inequality, Gini Coefficient, is lower in Scotland than might otherwise be expected. Scotland's Gini coefficient ranges from 0.36007 in Waves A–C and 0.33929 in Waves C–E. Thus, while **Table 5.2** highlights Scotland as maintaining an above average level of monthly household income, second only to that of the South of England, in relation to income inequality within Scotland, it lies below that of the South of England, the English Midlands and the North of England.

In summary, our descriptive data provides us with a picture of wide disparities both across the UK as a whole and within regions and nations in terms of average household income and inequality measures. The data generally highlights

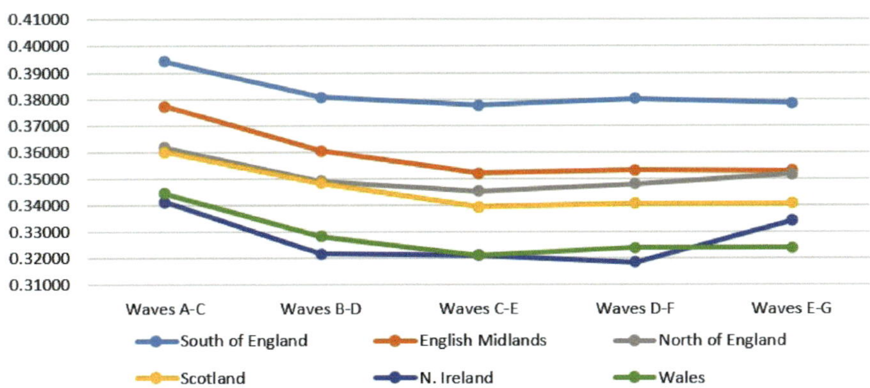

FIGURE 5.2 Regional and devolved nations Gini coefficients (three-year moving average)

that greater inequalities exist within higher-income regions and nations of the UK and the opposite can also be said of lower-income regions and nations. Poorer areas with lower levels of average household income (**Table 5.1** and **Figure 5.1**), also have lower levels of income inequality, as measured by their specific Gini coefficients (**Table 5.3** and **Figure 5.2**). These inequalities exist both between the different regions and nations of the UK as a whole (**Table 5.2** and **Figure 5.1**) and significantly within regions themselves (**Table 5.3** and **Figure 5.2**). This is most marked in the experience of Wales and northern Ireland where two devolved institutions have existed since the origins of the devolution era (**Table 5.3** and **Figure 5.2**).

This same relationship between inequality and devolution is more differentiated in areas of higher income and greater inequality areas of the UK; the experience of the South of England and that of Scotland differs markedly. The South of England has partially had a devolved institution, in the Greater London Authority since 2000, although this has had the least powers of all the devolved institutions. While the South of England confirms to the general pattern identified of high average household income associated with high measures of inequality, the same is not the case with Scotland. Thus, while Scotland has higher than average monthly household income (**Table 5.2** and **Figure 5.1**), it achieves a lower level of inequality compared to many other English regions with lower average household income (**Table 5.3** and **Figure 5.2**).

These initial findings appear to suggest a complex relationship exists between devolution and inequality. The literature linking fiscal devolution with increasing income inequality includes studies by Rodríguez-Pose and Ezcurra (2010) and Sacchi and Salotti (2014) that conclude that increased fiscal devolution increases rather than decreases income inequality between regions due to the inability to redistribute through fiscal transfers. As Sacchi and Salotti conclude, 'higher degree of autonomy and responsibility over taxes assigned to sub-central governments is associated with a more unequal distribution of income across households within a country' (2014, p. 218). However, the methodology in both studies focuses upon income inequality between regions, inter-regional inequality measured relative to that at the national level (Rodríguez-Pose and Ezcurra, 2010, pp. 19–44; Sacchi and Salotti, 2014, pp. 202–212). If we wish to examine the extent to which devolution impacts on inequality, we need to focus our attention upon within region inequalities, intra-regional inequality.

The only quantitative study of devolution and inequality in the UK to examine intra-regional inequality was undertaken by Morelli and Seaman (2007) using the British Household Panel Survey (BHPS), the forerunner of the UKHLS Understanding Society dataset. The BHPS data covered the period pre- and post-devolution with household surveys spanning the years 1991–1993 to 2001–2003 but, with around 10,000 households, involved a much smaller sample size compared to the UKHLS. Their examination of intra-regional inequality also found wide-ranging levels of regional and national income disparities and dispersion consistent with the relationship identified above for the UKHLS.

Morelli and Seaman (2007) also identified the high levels of average monthly income and income inequality found for Scotland. Using Ordinary Least Squares (OLS) regression analysis, they however, concluded that there was no statistically significant relationship linking devolution and income inequality. As they concluded for Scotland and Wales:

> [n]either Scotland nor Wales have been able to significantly improve upon the general trend of gently-declining intra-regional income inequality operating throughout most of the UK during this period, and it is difficult to detect any significant impact of devolution in this process.
>
> *(Morelli and Seaman, 2007, p. 535)*

It is possible to again test using OLS regression analysis with the UKHLS data to examine the robustness of this conclusion. Using our Gini coefficient as our dependent variable, we can regress average monthly household income to test for the statistical significance of the relationship between inequality and the existence of devolution (see Equation 5.1). In the case of the UKHLS data, we see (**Table 5.4**) below markedly differing results emerge:

$$GINI = \alpha(eNMHI) + \beta(Earned) + \mu(3child) + \Omega(Single) + \pi(Unemp) + \phi(country) + cons \quad \text{(Equation 5.1)}$$

Table 5.4 provides the regression results for the UKHLS data for the seven waves of data from Wave A (2010) to Wave G (2016) and covers 12 regions with dummy variables for the devolved administrations of Scotland, northern Ireland and Wales providing 84 data points. In addition, a series of variables are included to test for other determinants of income inequality. Average equivalised real monthly household income after housing costs (*eNMHI*), earned income (*Earned*)

TABLE 5.4 Regression Results of Correlation UKHLS eNMHI with UK Gini Coefficient

Variable	*Coefficient.*	*Std. Err.*	*t-stat*	*P> |t|*
eNMHI	.0000265	.0000127	2.09	0.040
Earned	.4699137	.0782387	6.01	0.000
Unemp	.0041108	.0014568	2.82	0.006
3 Child	.0226574	.0128444	1.76	0.082
Single	.0101824	.0293464	0.35	0.730
Scotland	−.0220511	.0075371	−2.93	0.005
northern Ireland	−.008797	.0082088	−1.07	0.287
Wales	−.0132861	.0076953	−1.73	0.088
Cons	−.0303631	.0575359	−0.53	0.599
Number of obs = 84				
R-squared = 0.5890				
Adj R-squared = 0.5451				

Source: UKHLS, Waves A–G (2010–2016).

and the unemployment rate (*Unemp*) all would be expected to be generate positively signed and significant correlation coefficients (α, β and π) in their relationship to income inequality measured in terms of the Gini coefficient (*Gini*) and acting as our determinant variable. Our expectation is that as average monthly household income, earned income or the unemployment rate rise, all act as key components of household income, they would all be both positively related and significant (a t-statistic value greater than +/− 1.97) in their relationship with income inequality.

The second determinant of income inequality and the Gini coefficient would we expect to be household size and, therefore, we include variables for large families (*3 Child*) and single adult (*Single*) households. We would expect large families to have a positive correlation coefficient (μ) with the Gini coefficient, while single adult household's correlation coefficient (Ω) has a negative correlation as larger households require higher income. Finally, our model includes dummy variables (*country*) for each of the three devolved administrations of Scotland, Wales and northern Ireland and are given the value 1, while all other 9 English regions take the value 0. All results are understood to be in comparison with the UK average level of income inequality, as measured by the Gini coefficient.

The results of our regression analysis demonstrate that the three income-related variables (*eNMHI*, *Earned* and *Unemp*) are indeed all positively signed in their coefficients and significant in their correlation with UK the Gini Coefficient. Equivalised real monthly household income net of housing costs (*eNMHI*) coefficient of 0.0000265 suggests a weak positive correlation but with a t-statistic = 2.09 is significant at the 5% level. In contrast, the variable for earned income (*Earned*), measured as a proportion of the regions income derived from labour income, has a high correlation 0.4699137 and a high statistical significance of t-statistic = 6.01. The unemployment rate (*Unemp*) is again positively signed (0.0041108) and significant at the 5% level (t-statistic = 2.82), suggesting that as unemployment rises, inequality rises similarly. Note that earned income (*Earned*) and unemployment rates (*Unemp*) impact on inequality in opposite ways. As earned income rises, those at the bottom of the income distribution are left behind in workless households, while in-work households income rises leading to increasing income inequality whereas when unemployment rates rise greater numbers fall into the lowest income levels, reliant upon welfare payments, leading to increasing income inequality as those remaining in-work maintain their living standards.

Our measures of the relationship of household types with income inequality (**Table 5.4**) demonstrate that a weaker correlation is in effect. Large families (*3Child*) are positively correlated with income inequality with a coefficient of .0226574 but with a t-statistic = 1.76 only significant at the 10% level confirming our knowledge in Chapter 3 that higher numbers of children are a determinant of low-income households. Single adult household (*Single*) by contrast while positively signed fails to be significant with a low t-statistic (0.35).

Most interestingly the results for the coefficients for the devolved institutions (Scotland, northern Ireland and Wales) all indicate negative correlations with income inequality suggesting that devolution does indeed reduce intra-regional income inequality but only in the case of Scotland (t-statistic = −2.93), is it significant at the 5% level while in Wales (t-statistic = −1.73) it is significant at the 10% level.

In the earlier 2007 study of BHPS data, Morelli and Seaman again found negative correlation coefficients for devolution for Scotland and Wales of the same magnitude of −0.02. However, in their 2007 study, none were statistically significant, although in the case of Scotland the t-statistic = −1.529 was close to 10% significance (Morelli and Seaman, 2007, Table 3). Now some two decade later, however, the Scotland correlation, at the 5% level, and the Welsh correlation, at the 10% level, indicate that devolution is indeed linked to reductions in intra-region income inequality. In the case of Scotland, by referring to **Figure 5.2** in the absence of devolution, we would expect the picture of income inequality to be higher. Whereas **Figure 5.2** shows that inequality in Scotland is below that of East Midlands and North of England in the absence of devolution, we would expect it to be much closer to the level of the South of England.

In conclusion, this chapter suggests that average monthly household income has wide variation across the UK. These inequalities exist both at the UK level, between regions (inter-regional inequalities) and within the UK regions and nations themselves (intra-regional inequalities) as measured by the Gini coefficient. These are subject to small changes over the time period covered by the UKHLS dataset and reinforce the conclusions of our earlier chapters. Inequality within the UK, its regions and devolved nations, is structurally linked to levels of poverty and that limited levels of re-distribution exist. However, the OLS results in this chapter highlight that where devolution, and specifically fiscal devolution, has emerged in Scotland and Wales, a statistically significant impact can be identified. This impact on inequality is identified with powers that act to support employment and reduce unemployment and thus contribute towards monthly household income net of housing costs.

Devolution has gained support across the UK over time and has extended beyond budgetary control over expenditure into fiscal policy, in its most developed forms of Scotland and to a lesser extent Wales. Evidence for within devolved nations (intra-inequality) suggests that this has indeed had a statistically significant impact on intra-regional household income inequality.

Our final chapter examining the UKHLS, now turns to explore the mechanisms that may be used to address poverty and income inequality, examining the extent to which policy, either at a UK national or devolved level, could potentially further reduce income inequality.

References

BBC. (2020), *Transport for Wales Rail Services To Be Nationalised*, BBC News, 22nd October 2020, available at https://www.bbc.co.uk/news/uk-wales-54635421 accessed 5th June 2021.

BBC. (2021), *Scotland's Train Operator ScotRail To Be nationalised*, BBC News, 18th March 2021, available at https://www.bbc.co.uk/news/uk-scotland-scotland-politics-56432919 accessed 5th June 2021.

Bromley, C. (2006), *Has Devolution Delivered?*, Edinburgh: Edinburgh University Press.

Brown, G. (1975), *The Red Paper on Scotland*, Edinburgh: EUSPB.

Centre for Social Justice. (2006), *Denying the Vulnerable a Second Chance Undervaluing Britain's Third Sector in the Fight against Poverty Third Sector Working Group State of the Nation Report*, London: Centre for Social Justice.

Holder, H., Robertson, R., Ross, S., Bennett, L., Gosling, J. and Curry, N. (2015), *Risk or Reward? The Changing Role of CCGs in General Practice*, London: Kings Fund, p. 5.

Holmwood, J., Hickey, T. and Wallis, S. (2016), The Alternative White Paper for Higher Education: In Defence of Public Higher Education: Knowledge for a Successful Society, available at https://heconvention2.files.wordpress.com/2016/06/awp1.pdf

Kay, A. (2003), Evaluating Devolution in Wales, *Political Studies* 51, pp. 51–66.

Keating, M. (2003), Social Inclusion, Devolution and Policy Divergence. *Political Quarterly* 74, pp. 429–438.

Keating, M. (2005), Policy Convergence and Divergence in Scotland under Devolution. *Regional Studies* 39, pp. 453–463.

Keating, M. (2017), Commentary Brexit and Devolution in the United Kingdom. *Politics and Governance* 5(2), pp. 1–3.

Kim, E., Hong, S.W. and Ha, S.J. (2003), Impact of National Development and Decentralization Policies on Regional Income Disparity in Korea. *Annals of Regional Science* 37, pp. 79–91.

Krugman, P. (1994), *Peddling Prosperity: Economic Sense and Nonsense in the Age of Diminished Expectations*, New York: W.W Norton and Company.

McCafferty, P. (2006), Safe in Their Hands? Understanding Health and Health Policy in the Devolved Scotland, in G. Mooney, T. Sweeney and A. Law (eds.), *Social Care: Health and Welfare in Contemporary Scotland*, Paisley: Kynoch and Blaney, pp. 195–214.

McGettigan, A. (2013), *The Great University Gamble and the Future for Higher Education*, London: Pluto Press.

Mooney, G. and Scott, G. (eds.) (2012), *Social Justice and Social Policy in Scotland*, Bristol: Policy Press.

Morelli, C. and Seaman, P. (2007), Devolution and Inequality: A Failure to Create a Community of Equals? *Transactions of the Institute of British Geographers* 32, pp. 523–538.

National Centre for Social Science Research. (2012), *British Social Attitudes Survey*, 30, available at http://www.bsa.natcen.ac.uk/latest-report/british-social-attitudes-30/devolution/constitutional-preferences.aspx accessed 3rd June 2018.

Northern Powerhouse Partnership. (2017), *First Report*, January, available at http://www.northernpowerhousepartnership.co.uk/media/1192/npp-report-final.pdf accessed 5th January 2020.

Pike, A., Andrés Rodríguez-Pose, A. and Tomaney, J. (2007). What Kind of Local and Regional Development and for Whom. *Regional Studies* 41(9), pp. 1253–1269.

Rodríguez-Pose, A. and Ezcurra, R. (2010), Does Decentralization Matter for Regional Disparities? A Cross-Country Analysis. *Journal of Economic Geography* 10, pp. 619–644.

Sacchi, A. and Salotti, S. (2014), The Effects of Fiscal Decentralization on Household Income Inequality: Some Empirical Evidence. *Spatial Economic Analysis* 9(2), pp. 202–222.

Scottish Centre for Social Science Research. (2015), *ScotCen's Scottish Social Attitudes Survey 2015*, available at http://scotcen.org.uk/media/1123185/ssa15-attitudes-to-government-tables-for-web.pdf accessed 3rd June 2018.

Scottish Government. (2016), *Scotland Act*, (2016), Part II, Section 13, available at http://www.legislation.gov.uk/ukpga/2016/11/section/13/enacted accessed 7th June 2018.

Scottish Government. (2017), Minster for Transport and Islands Briefing Note: Glasgow Prestwick Airport Meeting Thursday 8th June 2017, available at https://www.gov.scot/binaries/content/documents/govscot/publications/foi-eir-release/2017/10/

foi-17-02116/documents/foi-17-02116-glasgow-prestwick-airport-notes-briefing-paper-pdf/foi-17-02116-glasgow-prestwick-airport-notes-briefing-paper-pdf/govscot%3Adocument/FOI-17-02116%2BGlasgow%2BPrestwick%2BAirport%2BNotes%2Band%2BBriefing%2BPaper.pdf accessed 5th June 2021.

Sloman, J. (1997), *Economics* (3rd edition), Hemel Hampstead: Prentice Hall, pp. 690–691.

Stigler, G. (1957), The Tenable Range of Functions of Local Government, *Joint Economic Committee, Federal Expenditure Policy for Economic Growth and Stability*, Washington, DC: World Bank.

Stiglitz, J. (2002), *Globalisation and Its Discontents*, London: Penguin.

Tselios, V., Rodríguez-Pose, A., Pike, A.J., Tomaney, J. and Torrisi, G. (2012), Income Inequality, Decentralisation and Regional Development in Western Europe. *Environment and Planning A* 44(6), pp. 1278–1301.

UK Government. (2012), *Health and Social Care Act* (2012), available at http://www.legislation.gov.uk/ukpga/2012/7/contents/enacted accessed 5th June 2019.

UK Government. (2016), *Cities and Local Government Devolution Act (2016)*, available at https://web.archive.org/web/20160305010639/http://services.parliament.uk/bills/2015-16/citiesandlocalgovernmentdevolution.html accessed 3rd December 2019.

Varoufakis, Y. (2015), *The Global Minatour: America, Europe and the Future of the Global Economy*, London: Zed Books.

Wales Health and Social Care Department. (2005), *Designed for Life: Creating World Class Health and Social Care for Wales in the 21st Century*, Cardiff: Welsh Assembly.

6

CHILD POVERTY

Creating intergenerational poverty

Introduction

This chapter uses data from the UK Longitudinal Household Panel Study, Understanding Society (UKHLS), to examine the incidence of child poverty in the UK across multiple waves of data. It demonstrates a further advantage of the longitudinal household panel survey method, namely, the ability to utilise the dataset to demonstrate the impact on poverty and inequality of policy initiatives, targeting specific household characteristics over time. Child poverty is used to examine the geographical relationship between poverty and inequality and evaluate the impact of different methods of targeting welfare. The chapter provides a contrast between means-testing and universal benefits to demonstrate the effectiveness of universal welfare provision.

Previous chapters have demonstrated that the unique longitudinal aspect of the UKHLS provides for analysis following the same household overtime. As we highlighted in Chapter 3, this facilitated an examination of mobility within the lowest income decile of the population and specifically concluded that mobility out of extreme poverty is highly correlated with household characteristics. In doing so, the chapter identified that socially structured and institutionalised aspects of extreme poverty can be identified. Chapter 4 followed a similar approach, this time examining the wealthiest households at the top of the income distribution, and again showed the extent to which the higher up the income distribution a household was located the lower the extent of mobility. Again, the chapter identified specific socially determined structural characteristics of households within this part of the income distribution and that these characteristics were persistent over time. The UKHLS facilitates further investigation of poverty and inequality by using the geographical location of households to examine the impact of policy changes on inequality and poverty. In Chapter 5,

DOI: 10.4324/9781315179957-6

we examined the impact of devolution on inequality to investigate the potential for the existence of policy divergence impacting differentially on poverty and inequality within the UK. Here we found that devolution in Scotland and Wales was correlated with reductions in household poverty and inequality, and these correlations were statistically significant.

In this chapter, we now seek to further demonstrate the ability to use the UKHLS dataset to test for further evidence of the effect of policy focused interventions on poverty and inequality. Choosing child poverty as our focus of attention, in this chapter, we examine the incidence and geographic distribution of child poverty. In doing so, the chapter ensures that the analysis developed in previous chapters provides comparability in its methodological approach. However, it also allows for an extension of the analysis by introducing an examination of the advantages and disadvantages of policy focused initiatives to address inequality and poverty. Specifically, we contrast the use of universal welfare with means-tested welfare interventions for households facing child poverty.

Child poverty in the UK

The existence of children within a household has long been identified as a strong predictor of household poverty. William Beveridge's (1942) *Social Insurance and Allied Services* recognised child poverty as one of the key drivers of household poverty in the UK. Beveridge utilised a life-cycle model of poverty in which child rearing was a key period in which household incomes were likely to fall below levels required for a minimum subsistence level and 'want', one of the five great evils, prevailed (Beveridge, 1942, pp. 154–58). The introduction of the *Family Allowances Act, 1945*, brought in a universal cash payment contributing towards the raising of children payable for the second and subsequent children in a household. Of importance to the introduction of family allowances, as Beveridge (1942, p. 155) outlined, was that they should be non-contributory and independent of any insurance-based system of entitlement. Thus, universal provision was to be the basis for the development of welfare targeting child poverty within the newly formed welfare state (Fraser, 1989; Glennerster, 1990, pp. 11–27). While universality prevailed in relation to child poverty, contribution-based welfare continued to be the basis for other forms of welfare. The *Social Insurance and Allied Services* report formed the ideological basis for the post Second World War welfare state and Beveridge made the case for a continuation of insurance led contributions in many areas of support, particularly in relation to unemployment or 'idleness' in Beveridge's framework. The result would be more generous differential levels of entitlement for those who had contributed through insurance payments and means-tested assessments for those without sufficient contribution levels. Despite Government's continued commitment to an understanding of poverty arising from individual failure, with respect to child welfare, universality was at its guiding principle. Universal provision and entitlement was understood to protect those unable to engage in employment.

Children, in other words, could not exercise individual responsibility and gain insurance-based protection. Second, universality introduced an intergenerational linkage between younger and old generations such that systems of general taxation could be justified in order to provide the resources available for the payment of welfare (Crowther, 1988; Lowe, 1993). Thus, the costs of welfare would now fall on the general population rather than firms within the economy.

The impact of the *Family Allowance Act 1945* and other welfare reforms in the late 1940s was the marked reduction of child poverty through to the beginning of the 1970s with less than one in ten children living in poverty (Morelli and Seaman, 2005, p. 585). However, the reappearance of mass unemployment in the early 1970s again resulted in the return of extensive child poverty with over 1 million children identified as living in poverty. In response to this rise in child poverty, government extended universal welfare payments, following the passing of the *Child Benefit Act* 1975, for the first time now including payments to households for the first child.

Despite universal approaches to child poverty, the existence of means-testing for adult's receipt of welfare ensured that tensions between universality and means-testing were embedded into the welfare state and to be subject to continued discourse. This discourse could at times be confused by a loose use of terminology. Proponents of means-testing could base their view on a need to 'target' welfare support to more deserving groups within the population while ignoring the fact that universal welfare is a form of needs-based 'targeting' of welfare. Means-testing, therefore, replaced need with income as the mechanism utilised for targeting. Universal provision had avoided means-testing income as a mechanism for targeting in favour of other objective criteria, the existence of children in a household, in the case of child poverty, or the diagnosis of ill health in the case of provision of free health care at the point of need in the National Health Service (Stirling-Ross, 1952). This debate took on greater significance from the late 1970s onwards when the rising cost of welfare led to increasing moves to restrict welfare support (Hills, 1990: 1995). The original Beveridge insurance-based system of welfare support utilising a flat-rate National Insurance 'stamp' was replaced with a National Insurance payment linked to a percentage of income for those in employment following the introduction of the *Social Security Act* 1975 (Barr and Coulter, 1990, p. 278). Unemployment benefits for the insured unemployed were accompanied by a means-tested system of supplementary benefits available to those without access to insurance-based welfare. Supplementary benefits had their origins in the *Supplementary Benefits Act* 1966 and covered uninsured households, primarily the long-term unemployed, pensioners, single parents and those unable to work due to sickness. The second *Supplementary Benefits Act* 1976 continued with this means-tested mechanism for determining access to supplementary financial support into the welfare system (*Supplementary Benefits Act*, 1976, section 1). Together the *Social Security Act* 1975 and the *Supplementary Benefits Act* ensured levels of support for low-income households began to fall, marking a decisive shift away from the welfare state providing minimum standards of living to one in which welfare support from the 1980s onwards increasingly imposed absolute poverty upon those reliant on welfare for their income. Additionally, this different approach now began the process by which punitive sanctions were introduced on individuals in low-income households for failing to engage in seeking work as a route out of poverty (Clark, 1978).

The rising levels of worklessness in households, as mass unemployment rose into the 1980s, combined with reductions in the welfare support for households unable to access work lead to large scale increases in child poverty (Gregg, Harkness and Machin., 1999, pp. 163–87). A lack of employment opportunities, limited geographical mobility for families in relocating for work together with poor access to affordable childcare were persistently identified as barriers to workless households accessing labour markets as a route out of poverty (Banks and Johnson, 1993; Adelman, Ashworth and Middleton, 2000). Alongside the increasing participation of women in the labour market, there were marked changes in the demographics of households both in work and in poverty in the UK by the late twentieth century. For households with adults in work, the single wage-earning household was rapidly declining to be replaced by households with two wage earners. Between 1961 and 1991, single-wage-earning households fell by more than half from 68% of households to just 32% of households (Webb, 1995, Figure 2). This growing economic independence for women was also leading to further demographic changes occurring in how children were being reared with Hills (1993) reporting that single-parent households more than doubled from 8% of households to 19% from 1971 to 1991. Together welfare, labour market and demographic changes meant that child poverty became one of the defining characteristics of household poverty from the 1980s onwards. Data from the 1980s demonstrated these to be permanent structural changes in poverty rates within workless households with children. Through the 1990s and into the twenty-first century, the incidence of child poverty was as high as one in three households with children (Brewer, Clark and Goodman, 2003; Nickell, 2004).

The adoption of supply-side economic policies by successive governments through the 1980s and 1990s led to sharp changes in industrial structure, rising inequality and the geographical distribution of poverty (Dorling et al., 2007; Doogan, 2009; Piketty, 2014). This extended into welfare policy through an increasing conditionality being placed on households receiving welfare. Child poverty was exacerbated by this explicitly Malthusian ideology, reinvented from the Victorian era, which now sought to distinguish between a deserving and undeserving poor. Underpinned by monetarist economic arguments engagement in labour markets, and incentivising the mobility of human capital, 'work as a route out of poverty' provided the guiding principle of welfare reform (Dilnot, 1995, pp. 1–10). Unsurprisingly, those households least able to access work were those households most negatively impacted by labour market and welfare reforms in this period (Machin, 1996, pp. 47–64). Not until in-work benefits specifically targeting households with children emerged, in the form of Working Family Tax Credits, did labour markets and paid work provide a sustainable means for households with children to seek to avoid child poverty (Dorling, 2014, pp. 55–88). Indeed, as in-work benefits emerged as an anti-poverty strategy, adults in households experiencing child poverty demonstrated a rapidly rising responsiveness to labour market participation, such that the stigmatisation of adults in households with children in poverty as feckless and 'hard to reach' proved unfounded (Nickell, 2004).

Despite the responsiveness of households with children to participate in labour markets, child poverty continued at historically high levels into the twenty-first century. Although falling from its record levels of one in three households with children living in poverty child poverty relentlessly affected one in four households with children at any one time. A central explanation for this continued correlation between high labour market participation for adults and high poverty rates for households with children lay in the gendered nature of labour market participation available to adults in households with children. Part-time, low wage, low skill and precarious insecure work became defining features of the segmented labour markets available to adults in households with child care responsibilities (Wills, 2009, pp. 441–460). Despite high levels of education, high skill and experience women who left the workforce for childcare reasons were returning to lower-skilled and lower paid employment within the labour market (Beatty, Fothergill, Houston, Powell and Sissons, 2009, pp. 958–974). Flexibility of labour was not matched by flexibility of employers allowing those working part-time equal opportunity to career progression and higher-paid skilled work.

Evidence also emerged demonstrating that the experience of child poverty was much more widespread than the absolute level at any one point in time. High levels of mobility in and out of poverty for households with children suggested that while the absolute level remained high much larger numbers of households with children faced the experience and consequences of poverty. Low-income households with children were deemed to be particularly vulnerable to small changes in tax and benefit levels as their household income combined both employment and welfare income. Threshold levels for means-tested welfare created 'poverty traps' in which high marginal taxation rates led to sharp reductions in household's income with the consequential deleterious impact on children and their families (Goodwin, 2017).

The persistence of high child poverty rates meant that it became a key indicator of wider social well-being and a measure of progress or decline in the effectiveness of welfare policy both in the UK, and internationally as countries replicated changes to welfare policy adopted in the UK (Platt, 2005; Chen and Corak, 2008).

This chapter now turns to assess these issues through the examination of households with children in the UKHLS. The UKHLS defines children as those under 16 and provides information that permits household re-composition to take place. While all individuals are interviewed and their data collected separately, in the UKHLS, the data can be combined such that all individuals living within a single household can be linked together to create household-level data. In so doing, the household characteristic of having children living in the household can be used to examine the relationship between household size and geographical distribution, the extent of mobility of households with children in and out of the lower-income deciles and the impact of targeting child welfare support on household income.

Table 6.1 shows the descriptive statistics for the distribution of households and the number of children in households on an aggregated regional and national basis along with the UK levels for the dataset beginning with Wave B data collected in 2011. Thus, Wales and Scotland have the highest percentage of households in the data without children at 64.8% and 64.0% respectively, while conversely, the South of England and the North of England have the highest number of households with children at 42.0% and 40.8% respectively. The South of England and the North of England are also the areas with both the highest proportion of small households (with one child) and large households (four or more children) with 19.3% and 1.7% for the South of England and 19.0% and 1.8% for the North of England respectively. **Table 6.1** also provides average numbers of children per household to show comparison. Thus, the average number of children per household in each region shows large variations from 0.74 children per household in the South of England falling to only 0.59 children in households in Wales. However, the average number of children per household (excluding households without children) shows the differences are much less evident with the average number of children in households with children

TABLE 6.1 UKHLS Households with Children, Wave B (2011)

	Aggregated Regions and Nations						
No. of Children in Household	*South of England*	*Midlands*	*North of England*	*Scotland*	*northern Ireland*	*Wales*	*UK*
0	58.0%	60.8%	59.2%	64.0%	60.4%	64.8%	60.1%
1	19.3%	17.4%	19.0%	17.3%	18.4%	16.9%	18.4%
2	15.5%	15.3%	15.2%	13.9%	14.4%	13.1%	15.0%
3	5.4%	4.9%	4.8%	3.9%	5.32%	4.4%	4.9%
4 or more	1.7%	1.6%	1.8%	0.9%	1.6%	0.8%	1.6%
Total*	100%	100%	100%	100%	100%	100%	100%
Average number of children per household	0.7431	0.6965	0.7162	0.6046	0.6945	0.5946	0.6990
Average number children in households (excluding households without children)	1.7693	1.7771	1.7537	1.6790	1.7547	1.6908	1.7540

Source: UKHLS Wave B (2011). Children refers to the age range of 0–15 inclusive. Adult 'children' (> = 16 years) are not counted since they are considered to be 'adults' in the UKHLS.

* Some totals do not add to 100 due to rounding errors.

ranging from 1.78 children per household in the Midlands falling to 1.68 in Scotland. Our final column provides the average for each household category for the dataset as a whole.

The picture emerging from the descriptive data suggests that while there is some variation between regions and nations in the UK, the variation is limited with no apparent highly specific differences clearly evident. However, once these household distributions are linked to income levels greater dispersion becomes more evident. As noted in previous chapters, comparing households of differing sizes with incomes requires a recognition that households of different sizes require different levels of income for similar living standards and we, therefore, need to use an equivalence scale to ensure comparability between households (Jenkins, 1988; Lambert, 2001). This is particularly important where households contain children and therefore the household is likely to incur greater costs for a comparable standard of living. While a variety of equivalence scales are available to use, they all have the same property, namely that larger household's income is reduced relative to smaller households to recognise the higher income required for comparable living standards (Aarberge and Melby, 1998). The McClements Scale, as described in Chapter 2, is the most widely used equivalence scale used for this purpose and the one adopted in all of the analyses in this volume.

In **Table 6.2**, we see the impact on household income for households when we equivalise income levels. Again, for consistency, we have used equivalised real monthly household income net of housing costs as the measure of household income (eNHMI). **Table 6.2** shows that a single child household's average monthly income declines from a nominal £2,886 to an equivalised £2,478, a 14% reduction, after the relative additional costs of including one child in a household relative to the income of a household without children. As can be seen in **Table 6.2** the changes to household income for two, three and four or more children highlight the level of reductions occurring as a result of the use of

TABLE 6.2 UKHLS Equivalised Monthly Household Income Net of Housing Costs eNMHI, Wave B (2011)

	Number of Children in Household				
Average Income	*1*	*2*	*3*	*4 or More*	*All Households*
Non-equivalised household income	£2,886	£2,938	£2,695	£2,195	£2,983
Equivalised household income	£2,478	£2,684	£2,473	£1,883	£2,495
Percentage of with children households found in Decile 1	8.59%	7.41%	7.29%	10.24%	
Percentage of with children households found in Deciles 2 & 3	16.64%	13.26%	15.54%	11.08%	
Percentage of with children households in deciles 1–3	25.23%	20.67%	22.83%	21.32%	

Source: UKHLS Wave B (2011).

equivalence scales. **Table 6.2** further highlights the extent of child poverty by highlighting the proportion of the households with children found in the lowest income decile and then the second and third lowest income deciles. Thus, for households with one child 8.59% are located in the lowest income decile while a further 16.64% are found in the second- and third-income deciles. Together the data shows that some 25.23% of all households with one child have equivalised income levels that place them in the poorest 30% of households. For all other households with children, the table shows that over 20% of these families are also in the poorest 30% of households.

The UKHLS data confirms what is widely known about child poverty in the UK (Dorling, 2010, pp. 36–45; McKendrick, Mooney, Dickie, Scott and Kelly, 2014, pp. 114–135). A high level of child poverty is evident. Between one in four and one in five households with children live in the poorest 30% of households. However, it is not simply the high levels of child poverty that is important. This picture of high levels of child poverty needs to be examined dynamically in relation to the experience of child poverty. Again, as highlighted in earlier chapters, it is the longitudinal design of the UKHLS that facilitates the examination to which the existence of child poverty may be understood as a transitory or permanent feature of children's life experience. **Table 6.3** uses the initial dataset in Wave B (2011) to test for evidence of longevity of child poverty for households with children. Again, this follows our standard approach to examining mobility used in Chapters 3 and 4 earlier.

In **Table 6.3**, we initially observe the percentage of households with children who have moved from the lowest income decile in Wave B (2011) by Waves C to G (2012–2016) compared with those households without children. Thus, after 12 months, between Waves B and C, some 56% of households without children have left the lowest income decile. The comparable figure for households with children is 64.2% and for all households combined the figure is 57.9%. Examining the percentages in subsequent waves of the data, Waves D–G, we

TABLE 6.3 UKHLS Mobility for Households with Children, Waves B–G, 2011–2016

	Exit from the Decile 1			*Exit from Deciles 1–3*		
By Which Wave Did the Exit Occur?	*Households without Children*	*Households with Children*	*All Households*	*Households without Children*	*Households with Children*	*All Households*
By Wave C	56.0%	64.2%	57.9%	31.0%	44.3%	34.1%
By Wave D	18.5%	15.7%	17.8%	14.2%	15.6%	14.5%
By Wave E	7.5%	8.8%	7.8%	8.9%	8.7%	8.9%
By Wave F	6.7%	3.8%	6.0%	7.8%	7.6%	7.7%
By Wave G	3.0%	5.0%	3.5%	5.3%	4.2%	5.0%
Remain in the bottom decile	8.3%	2.5%	6.9%	32.9%	19.6%	29.7%

Source: UKHLS Waves B–G (2011–2016).

can conclude that overall, households with children appear to demonstrate more mobility than households without children for the very poorest households, those in the bottom income decile. Thus, by Wave G (2016), five years after households appeared in the bottom decile just 2.5% of households with children remain in the bottom decile compared to 8.3% of households without children. While this suggests extreme poverty, living in a household in the lowest 10% of all household incomes, is a transient experience for all but a small proportion of households with children, possibly due to a temporary economic shock to the household, it also implies that many more children have had this experience of extreme poverty than we might otherwise consider.[1]

The optimistic interpretation of this evidence of movement out of the lowest income decile is also somewhat tempered by the examination of the experience of households with children in the lowest three income deciles. The second part of **Table 6.3** evidences a broadly similar, albeit lower, pattern of mobility for households with children in the bottom three income deciles as found in the lowest income decile. Thus, as noted above, while 64.2% of households with children had left the bottom income decile after 12 months (between Waves B and C) the comparable figure for households with children in the bottom three income deciles is 44.3%. Similarly, for households without children, the comparable figures are 56% compared to 31% respectively.

However, overall lower levels of mobility are more starkly found for those households in the lowest three income deciles after five years than for the lowest income decile. Between Waves B and G (2011 and 2016), the numbers remaining in the lowest three income deciles for households with children is 19.6% alongside 32.9% for households without children compared to the figures of 2.5% and 8.3% respectively within the lowest income decile. The proportion of households with children remaining in prolonged poverty remain almost eight times that of households in extreme poverty in the very bottom income decile. **Table 6.3** thus indicates that while households with children have access to sufficient income, through work of social security benefits, to lift them out of the experience of the extreme poverty of the very lowest income decile this income is insufficient to lift them out of the experience of the prolonged poverty of living in households in the bottom 30% of households of the income distribution. Further, this experience of prolonged poverty, lasting at least five years, accounts for almost 20% of all households with children.

Such high levels and such prolonged experiences of child poverty has, as discussed above, led social reformers since Beveridge to seek to address the specific impact of poverty on children (Le-Grand, 1990; Benzeval, Taylor and Judge, 2000; Department for Work and Pensions, 2002). A key feature of these debates has been over the mechanism to deliver welfare to children and the use of means-tested versus utilising universal benefits (Atkinson, 2015). Here again, we can use the UKHLS dataset to assess the impact a notional increase in household income would have for households with children relative to all other households. In order to examine the potential impact of a change in means-testing over a universal provision of welfare, we need to consider how different policy options impact household incomes.

Household income is reported in the UKHLS dataset both in terms of earned income, namely income from employment, and income transfers derived from welfare payments of different kinds.[2] Once household income has been derived it is possible to add to those incomes based upon adjusting one or other of these income sources. Thus, it is possible to change the level of income from a particular welfare benefit, or combination of benefits, to reflect how a change in benefit levels could impact those specific households with children that receive the designated benefit(s). In so doing, we would be conceptually following a means-testing approach in which the level of the specific benefit changes while maintaining entitlement to the benefit remains constant. Thus, the existing means-testing assessment for each household with children remains static while the benefit level itself increases. One strong reason for taking this approach would be that the level of benefit(s) being adjusted is too low to address child poverty.

An alternatively conceptual approach would be to retain a constant level of benefit but adjust the extent of entitlement for household's access to the benefit itself. Here an increase in household income mirrors the increasing liberalisation of welfare receipt to reflect the introduction of a universal form of benefit. One strong reason for undertaking this approach would be that it is felt that the current benefit(s) inadequately target the desired population group and that child poverty would be better addressed by targeting a wider section of households with children.

Both adjustments would retain the concept of targeted benefits, directed to households with children, but one would follow a means-testing approach identifying households with existing entitlement to a means-tested benefit while the other utilises a universal approach identifying the existence of children in a household as the criteria for entitlement.

Free school meals

Free school meals are one child-centred policy option that has been the centre of debate for targeting food poverty, educational under-attainment and poor health outcomes in contemporary Britain (Scottish Government, 2003, p. 2004). The recognition of the UK's poor performance in addressing childhood poverty against other European economies led to a growing interest in concept of inter-generational poverty; an understanding that childhood poverty, rising levels of childhood obesity and diet-related ill-health were combining together such that the current generation of children being the first potentially to have a life expectancy lower than their parents (Machin., 1996; Gregg, Harkness and MacMillan, 1999; Nickell, 2004). This, combined with recognition of an increasing educational failure of children from poorer backgrounds placed child-focused welfare at the heart of contemporary welfare debates within the UK (Benzeval,

TABLE 6.4 Impact on Inequality in the Use of Free School Meals, UKHLS Wave B (2011)

Provision	*Gini Coefficient*	*Change in Gini Coefficient**
No free school meals	0.35067	
Trigger benefits: Income Support & Job Seekers Allowance (current system)	0.35027	−0.00040
Trigger benefits: As previous row plus working tax credits	0.34942	−0.00125
Trigger benefits: As previous row plus disability benefits	0.34941	−0.00126
Trigger benefits: As previous row plus Council Tax Benefit	0.34941	−0.00126
Trigger benefits: As previous row plus Housing Benefit	0.34940	−0.00127
Universal Free School Meals	0.34951	−0.00116

Source: UKHLS Wave B (2011).

* *Relative to no free school meals provision.*

Taylor and Judge, 2000; Gillborn and Kirkton, 2000; Wrigley, 2003; Ludbrook, Theodossiou and Gerova, 2005). For the purposes of this chapter, free school meals has additional advantages as a policy initiative for while reflecting a small income change to a household, it is nevertheless one which targets children directly, can be quantified in relation to its contribution to additional income to households on the basis of the individual cost of a meal and the number of days per year it is provided in school and finally, has defined criteria for its existing eligibility in relation to receipt of welfare, namely the receipt of Income Support and Job Seekers Allowance.[3]

In **Table 6.4**, we provide the Gini coefficient as the chosen measure of the level of inequality to assess the extent to which inequality decreases as the income of households with children are adjusted, to replicate the additional income arising from the introduction of free school meals. As discussed in Chapter 2, the lower the Gini coefficient, the more equal an income distribution is considered to be (Atkinson, 1980).

The second column provides the Gini coefficient for each of the methods of targeting free school meals to households with children, while the third column provides the change relative to the baseline of no provision of free school meals. Thus, the first example, the removal of existing free school meals, has the highest Gini coefficient at 0.35067. The introduction of a means-tested criteria and all subsequent extensions of provision reported show lower Gini coefficients and thus provide greater equality. Subsequent extensions of provision beyond the existing eligibility criteria of receipt of Income Support and Job Seekers Allowance reduces inequality to a minimum of 0.34940 when working family tax credits, disability benefits, council tax benefits and housing benefits are all included as gaining entitlement for free school meals. This contrasts with the Gini coefficient for a fully universal provision of 0.34951.

If our objective was to minimise income inequality through a measurement of the Gini coefficient the utilisation of means-testing with increasing liberal eligibility criteria for related child-welfare benefits such as free school meals would achieve this outcome in contrast to universal provision. This conclusion is, however, expected as an outcome of statistical nature of the Gini coefficient as a measure related to the whole of the income distribution. Any additional income allocated to the highest income households in a distribution will increase rather than decrease a measure of inequality. However, there may be other factors that together favour the provision of universal provision despite this outcome. The first, as noted by Beveridge previously, links inter-generational outcomes to welfare provision and acts to facilitate the wider support for the provision of welfare through general taxation. Thus, the existence of universal welfare provision encourages support for a broader level of redistribution within the welfare system.

Second, although more liberal entitlement within a means-tested system produces a lower level of income inequality, it does not result in all targeted groups being able to access the welfare provision. Those households unable to access welfare benefits giving entitlement to the additional benefits, in this case free school meals, leave many low-income households with children excluded from accessing free school meals (Katungi, Neale and Barbour, 2006). Households may be unable to access welfare for a wide variety of reasons ranging from complexity of the application process in the benefit system, social stigma in receiving benefits or discrimination preventing access to benefits individuals may be entitled to.

Figure 6.1 shows the proportion of the households captured by the increasingly liberal inclusion of benefits for accessing free school meals.

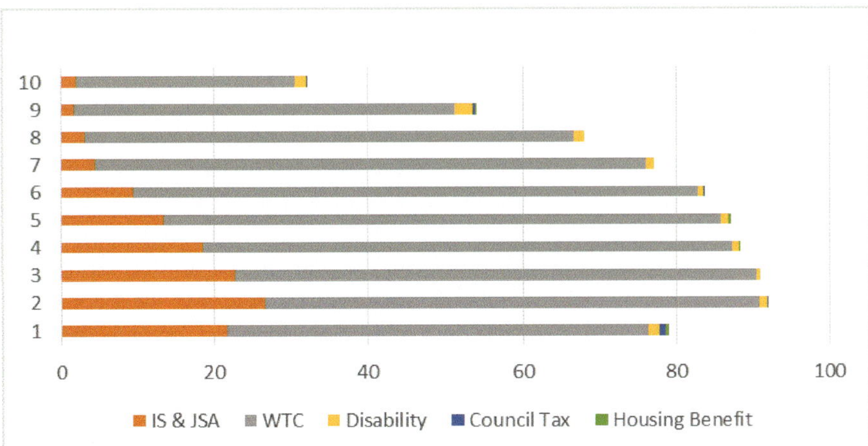

FIGURE 6.1 Percentage of households with children eligible for free school meals by expanding the range of benefits by income decile

Figure 6.1 shows the percentages of households on the horizontal axis in income deciles 1 to 10 on the vertical axis that would have access to free school meals based upon receipt of specific welfare benefits. Thus, under the current criteria of receipt of Income Support and Job Seekers Allowance (orange bar), less than 30% of households with children are successfully targeted in any income decile. Expanding the number of benefits granting entitlement to free school meals beyond the current criteria to include the most liberal entitlement, including Working Families Tax Credits, Disability benefits, Council Tax Benefit and Housing Benefit fails to target many of the most vulnerable and poorest households with children. Only 78% of households with children in the lowest income decile gain eligibility. This reaches a maximum of 92% of households in the second lowest income decile before falling rapidly beyond the six-income decile. Free school meals, as with all means-tested forms of welfare is affected a high prevalence of non-take-up of benefits. Households either do not or cannot claim specific benefits due to complexity of the welfare application process, criteria for assessment excluding household types or a resistance to increasingly behavioural conditionality for households in entitlement criteria. The extent of non-take-up of benefits is suggested by the Child Poverty Action Group to affect as many as one in five households (Child Poverty Action Group, 2005).

This is in contrast to universal provision where take-up is close to full coverage of the population. Thus, in seeking to ensure take-up of a child benefit is high the existence of universal provision is preferable. A particular aspect of non-take-up related to free school meals is the specific role played by stigma towards children identified as being in receipt of benefits. Pilot studies of breakfast club provision and free school meals in Scotland and local authorities evidenced the increased take-up where universal provision was the method of delivery (Scottish Government, 2003).

A final feature of differences between means-testing and universal provision is the expenditure on the cost of administration. Administration costs of means-tested benefits are order of magnitude higher than for universal provision due to the increasing complexities of the welfare system over time.

While our examination of the impact of increasing welfare demonstrates that universality provides advantages to means-testing as a mechanism for the delivery of welfare benefits to targeted populations, there is a further aspect of welfare provision that is also of relevance and was addressed in Chapter 5 examining devolution and the geographic aspects of inequality. As Chapter 5 demonstrated, the UKHLS facilitates disaggregation of the UK data into a limited number of large regions and nations within the UK. In so doing, it allows for a comparative assessment of UK policy on regional administrations and devolved nation's governments. **Table 6.5** highlights the geographic impact on inequality, again using our measure of the Gini coefficient, to show that areas of the UK with the highest levels of inequality are also those areas of the UK that see the largest reduction in inequality from a move towards universal provision.

Thus, the South of England and the Midlands both with the highest starting measure of inequality, with a Gini coefficient of 0.36457 and 0.36253 respectively

TABLE 6.5 Changes in UKHLS Gini Coefficient from a Move to Universal Provision – Mega-Region Disaggregation, Wave B (2011)

Provision	*UK*	*South of England*	*Midlands*	*North of England*	*Scotland*	*northern Ireland*	*Wales*
Current system	0.35027	0.36457	0.36253	0.33741	0.32001	0.30821	0.31907
Universal system	0.34951	0.36369	0.36172	0.33662	0.31970	0.30771	0.31851
Change in Gini	−0.00076	−0.00088	−0.00081	−0.00079	−0.00031	−0.00050	−0.00056

Source: UKHLS Wave B (2011).

Note: An analysis of Wave G data highlights similar results so is not displayed here but is available from the author on request.

are the two regions with the largest fall in inequality with a fall in Gini coefficient of 0.00088 and 0.00081 respectively. Conversely, those devolved administrations and UK nations and with the lowest measures of inequality see the lowest falls in inequality in the move towards universality. Thus, Wales, followed by northern Ireland and Scotland see the lowest falls in Gini coefficient of 0.00056, 0.00050 and 0.00031 respectively.

Conclusion

This chapter has sought to examine the potential for policy analysis using the UKHLS in relation to child poverty in the UK. Specifically, the longitudinal aspect of the UKHLS allows for changes in equality-related outcomes, at the level of the household, to be examined over time. In doing so the UKHLS allows for a comparative analysis of two distinct forms of welfare provision, means-testing versus universal provision, to be assessed. In the example chosen, of free school meals, the chapter highlighted the inability to target all households with children for a specific policy, such as free school meal provision through means-tested provision. This is identified as due to barriers in the ability of existing welfare recipients in low-income households to access entitlement of existing welfare benefits. Complexity in the administration of welfare, non-take-up of benefits and stigma all contribute to the reduced access to welfare by low-income households. Universal provision on the other hand has the ability to facilitate higher levels of take-up and participation by low-income households.

The chapter also highlighted two features evident in earlier chapters, namely the existence of structural inequality and poverty. Household characteristics again are shown to determine outcomes for households. Household with children is one form of household structure that continues to be highly correlated with poverty, inequality and a lack of mobility in the UK. Finally, the chapter's analysis also reinforces the recognition that UK-wide policy has marked and significant geographical differences in its impact. These differences provide policymakers with further opportunities to utilise welfare as a means of addressing regional and national inequalities within the UK.

Notes

1 Readers may recall that in Chapter 3, single parents in London were the only with children household typology that was significantly more likely to be in the bottom income decile.
2 The UKHLS also provides data on un-earned income, namely returns on saved income or assets. While this was important for the analysis in Chapter 4, for the purposes of this chapter, we can ignore this source of income.
3 The average cost of a free school meal in England was £1.93 in 2011 (the year of the UKHLS's Wave B), source https://www.bbc.co.uk/news/education-18873020 accessed 1st July 2020. UK Government legislation requires schools to open for a minimum 190 days per year. Source https://commonslibrary.parliament.uk/research-briefings/sn07148/ accessed 1st July 2020. Thus, the benefit of a free school meal can be set at (£1.93 x 190) / 12 (i.e., £30.56) per month per child.

References

Aarberge, R. and Melby, I. (1998), The Sensitivity of Income Inequality To Choice of Equivalence Scales. *Review of Income and Wealth Series* 44(4), December, pp. 556–569.

Adelman, L., Ashworth, K. and Middleton, S. (2000), Child Poverty in Britain, in (ed.). *Poverty and Social Exclusion in Britain*, York: Joseph Rowntree Foundation.

Atkinson, A.B. (1980), *Wealth, Income and Inequality* (2nd edition), Oxford: Oxford University Press.

Atkinson, A.B. (2015), *Inequality: What can Be Done?* London: Harvard University Press.

Banks, J. and Johnson, P. (1993), *Children and Household Living Standards*, London: Institute of Fiscal Studies.

Barr, N. and Coulter, F. (1990), Social Security: Solution or Problem?, in J. Hills (ed.), *The State of Welfare: The Welfare State in Britain Since 1974*, Oxford: Clarendon Press.

Beatty, C., Fothergill, S., Houston, D., Powell, R. and Sissons, P. (2009). A Gendered Theory of Employment, Unemployment and Sickness. *Environment and Planning C* 27(6), pp. 958–974.

Benzeval, M., Taylor, J. and Judge, K. (2000). Evidence on the Relationship between Low Income and Poor Health: Is the Government Doing Enough? *Fiscal Studies* 21(3), pp. 375–399.

Beveridge, W. (1942), *Social Insurance and Allied Services, CMD 6404–1942*, London: HMSO.

Brewer, M., Clark, T. and Goodman, A. (2003), What Really Happened to Child Poverty in the UK Under Labour's First Term?, *Economic Journal* 113, pp. 24–257.

Chen, W.H. and Corak, M. (2008). Child Poverty and Changes in Child Poverty. *Demography* 45(3), pp. 537–553. Published By: Duke University Press

Child Poverty Action Group. (2005), *First Steps to Reform Tax Credits*, London: CPAG.

Clark, M. (1978), The Unemployed on Supplementary Benefit: Living Standards and Making Ends Meet on a Low Income. *Journal of Social Policy* 7(4), pp. 385–410. doi:10.1017/S0047279400008151

Crowther, A. (1988), *British Social Policy 1914–39*, London: MacMillan.

Department for Work and Pensions. (2002), *Households Below Average Income 1994/5–2001/2*, London: Office of National Statistics.

Dilnot, A. (1995), The Assessment: The Future of the Welfare State'. *Oxford Review of Economic Policy* 1(3), pp. 1–10.

Doogan, K. (2009), *New Capitalism? The Transformation of Work*, Cambridge: Polity Press.

Dorling, D. (2010), *Injustice: Why Social Inequality Persists*, London: Pluto Press.

Dorling, D. (2014), *Inequality and the 1%*,, London: Verso Press.

Dorling, D., Rigby, J., Wheeler, B., Ballas, D., Thomas, B., Fahmy, E., Gordon, D. and Lupton, R. (2007), *Poverty, Wealth and Place in Britain, 1968 to 2005*, York: Joseph Rowntree Foundation.

Fraser, D. (1989), *The Evolution of the Welfare State* (2nd edition), London: MacMillan.

Gillborn, D. and Kirkton, A. (2000), White Heat: Racism, Under-Achievement and White Working-Class Boys. *International Journal of Inclusive Education* 4(4), pp. 271–288.

Glennerster, H. (1990), Social Policy Since the Second World War, in J. Hills (ed.), *The State of Welfare: The Welfare State in Britain Since 1974*, Oxford: Clarendon Press.

Goodwin, M. (2017), *The Parent Trap: Childcare Cuts Under Universal Credit, Children's Society*, London: Children's Society.

Gregg, P., Harkness, S. and Machin., S. (1999), Poor Kids: Trends in Child Poverty in Britain, 1968–96, *Fiscal Studies* 20, pp. 163–87.

Hills, J. (ed.) (1990), *The State of Welfare: The Welfare State in Britain Since*, Oxford: Clarendon Press.

Hills, J. (1993), *The Future of the Welfare State: A Guide to the Debate*, York: Joseph Rowntree Foundation.

Hills, J. (1995), Funding the Welfare State. *Oxford Review of Economic Policy* 1(3), pp. 27–43.

Jenkins, S. (1988), Reranking and the Analysis of Income redistribution. *Scottish Journal of Political Economy* 35(February), pp. 65–76.

Kakwani, N.C. (1977), Measurement of Tax Progressivity: An International Comparison. *Economic Journal* 87(March), pp. 71–80.

Kakwani, N.C. (1984), On the Measurement of Tax Progressivity and Redistributive Effect of Taxes with Applications to Horizontal and Vertical Equity. *Advances in Econometrics* 3, pp. 149–68.

Katungi, D., Neale, E. and Barbour, A. (2006), *People in Low-Paid Informal Work 'Need Not Greed*, York: Joseph Rowntree Foundation.

Lambert, P.J. (2001), *The Distribution and Redistribution of Income: A Mathematical Analysis* (3rd. edition), Manchester: Manchester University Press.

Le-Grand, J. (1990), The State of Welfare, in J. Hills (ed.), *The State of Welfare: The Welfare State in Britain Since 1974*, Oxford: Clarendon Press.

Lowe, R. (1993), *The Welfare State Since 1945*, New York: St. Martin's Press.

Ludbrook, A., Theodossiou, I. and Gerova, V. (2005), Health and Deprivation, in J.F. Ermisch and R E. Wright (eds.), *Changing Scotland: Evidence from the British Household Panel Survey*, Bristol: Policy Press.

Machin, S. (1996), Wage Inequality in the UK. *Oxford Review of Economic Policy* 7(1), pp. 47–64.

McKendrick, J., Mooney, G., Dickie, J., Scott, J. and Kelly, P. (2014), *Poverty in Scotland: The Independence Referendum and Beyond*, London: Child Poverty Action Group.

Mooney, G. and Scott, G. (eds.), (2004), *Exploring Social Policy in the 'New' Scotland*, Bristol: Policy Press.

Morelli, C.J. and Seaman, P. (2005), Universal Versus Targeted Benefits: The Distributional Effects of Free School meals. *Environment and Planning C: Government and Policy* 23, pp. 583–598.

Nickell, S. (2004), Poverty and Worklessness in Britain. *Economic Journal* 114, pp. 1–25

Piketty, T. (2014), *Capital in the Twenty First Century*, Cambridge, MA: Belknap Press of Harvard University Press.

Platt, L. (2005), *Studies in Poverty Inequality and Social Exclusion*, Bristol: Bristol University Press.

Scottish Government. (2003), *Hungry for Success: A Whole School Approach to School Meals in Scotland*, Edinburgh. Scottish Government.

Scottish Government. (2004), School Meals in Scotland, *National Statistics Bulletin, Education Series*, Edinburgh. Scottish Government.

Stirling-Ross, J. (1952), *The National Health Service in Great Britain*, Oxford: University Press.

Webb, S. (1995), Social Security Policy in a Changing Labour Market. *Oxford Review of Economic Policy* 11(3), pp. 11–26.

Wills, J. (2009), Subcontracted Employment and Its Challenge to Labor. *Labor Studies Journal* 34(4), pp. 441–460.

Wrigley, T. (2003), *Schools of Hope: A New Agenda for School Improvement*, Stoke-on-Trent: Trentham Books.

7

CONCLUSION

An evidence-based policy agenda for ending poverty

Introduction

The origin of this book lay in the opportunity to demonstrate the advantages of applying longitudinal panel data to the subject of poverty, wealth and inequality. As researchers in the area both authors wished to utilise the development of the Understanding Society, UK Household Longitudinal Study (UKHLS), to highlight its relevance to a wider audience of students, researchers and policymakers.

Our interest in poverty, wealth and inequality arises from the need to develop socially relevant research and apply economically informed analysis to the question of policy development. In doing so the UKHLS provides an evidence base arising from representative large datasets.

The UKHLS with over 40,000 individuals included is sufficient for both aggregation into household units and subsequent disaggregation into income deciles, household characteristics and geographical location without losing its representativeness.

The chapters of this book provide a methodological structure to research which is replicable and reproducible within the research community in Chapter 2. With the use of a small number of statistical techniques within a rigorous economic framework, longitudinal datasets can elucidate complex social relationships.

Chapters 3 and 4 provided an evidence base for the location of both poverty and wealth within a socially structured context, determined by the particular construction of poverty and wealth found in the UK. Together these chapters highlight the importance of recognising that poverty cannot be addressed without examining wealth and a requirement to consider the whole of the income distribution. They demonstrate that the conceptualisation of Malthusian deserving and undeserving poverty is unwarranted and hinders our understanding of the construction of poverty.

DOI: 10.4324/9781315179957-7

Chapters 5 and 6 then provide examples of how these structural features of poverty and wealth can be addressed in order to address levels of inequality. Chapter 5 examines the role of decentralised decision-making for social policy and anti-poverty strategies by highlighting the statistically significant correlations with devolution in Wales and Scotland. Importantly, we conclude that inequality varies across the nations and regions of the UK but that there is evidence of the impact of the devolution of governmental powers to devolved nations having a redistributive outcome on inequality. Chapter 6 focused upon the relevance of universality against means-testing for the development of targeted welfare support. Using the example of child poverty and the policy initiative of Free School Meals, the chapter demonstrates the advantages of universality for the ability to overcome barriers to inclusion from non-take-up of benefits. The chapter concludes that universality provides significant advantages over the continuation of means-testing for the provision of targeted benefits in the welfare system.

Together the chapters provide indications of how large longitudinal datasets can provide campaign groups, third sector organisations and policymakers with insights into the nature of poverty and equality in the form of representative samples.

There are many other examples of poverty and inequality that this book has not addressed to which the UKHLS can equally provide an evidence base, not least in terms of race with the addition of a sub-sample of BAME respondents. Thus, this book should not be understood as a final word on the matter in relation to the UKHLS, rather we hope it encourages others to begin to use this rich dataset.

Finally, in conclusion, if research is to address poverty and inequality, the totality of the income distribution requires a focus of attention. At the same time, social policy requires the development of evidenced-based research in which longitudinal analysis of representative samples contributes. With the United Kingdom Longitudinal Household Study panel dataset, we have one such resource in which these two goals of research on poverty is an important, yet underutilised, asset.

INDEX

For Product Safety Concerns and Information please contact our EU representative GPSR@taylorandfrancis.com Taylor & Francis Verlag GmbH, Kaufingerstraße 24, 80331 München, Germany